A
DATE
WITH
DEATH:
REDEMPTION

TOBY L. WILLIAMS

Evanescent Publishing, LLC

A DATE WITH DEATH: REDEMPTION

© 2018 EVANESCENT PUBLISHING COMPANY

WRITTEN BY TOBY L. WILLIAMS

EDITED BY KRISTEN JADE JENKINS

COVER ART BY CARL NAPOLEAN

"I DO NOT FEAR DEATH...

I FEAR THE LIFE THAT FOLLOWS,

THAT I WILL AWAKE TO AN ETERNAL FATE IN AN UNKNOWN REALM...

THAT IS WHAT QUICKENS ME.

FOR I DO NOT FEAR DEATH...

I FEAR THE LIFE THAT FOLLOWS."

-KRISTEN JADE.

CHAPTER I

DANCING THOUGHTS OF YESTERDAY.

Many thoughts of yesterday danced upon the floor of my mind as I gazed upon the path of my final destination.

I was being hauled like cargo to the fate of my tomorrow, still attached to yesterday's transgressions.

Transgression attached to regret, and regret accompanied by sorrow.. and rejection.. and abandonment, and tears, and inexplicable heartache.

For as long as I can remember, I have travelled the long, dark road of life in no particular direction, trusting the instinct of fear to evade certain occurrences.

Yet here I was, animalistically chained in the backseat of an unmarked police vehicle as proof that yesterday had ferociously hammered its way into my today, and intended to destroy my tomorrow.

 What dreams are there left to dream? What hope is there to keep alive?

Death is now approaching…

And deep within me lies the desire to embrace it.

The thoughts that haunt me welcome it.

I've stood alone at the cliff of death on many occasions in my life, but never have I had assistance to make sure I saw it through.

The prison corridors were crowded with men in white clothing. They all grew silent when they noticed me. I was being escorted in handcuffs, by two guards to an area where other men had experienced what I experienced earlier during the day— the dreadful tone of a judge's voice announcing a future procedure in death.

"We're going to two row," one of the guards announced to an officer controlling the cell doors.

The wing houses approximately sixty people with about twenty people on each row. There are three rows per wing.

"Eighteen," one of the escorting officers announced when we reached our destination.

Once relieved of my handcuffs, I immediately proceeded to the light located on the back wall of the 6 X 10ft. cell. My nostrils were attacked upon entrance from the smell of it.

Facing the back of the cell, to the left, there was a dirty white sink attached to the wall that required the push of a button for water to run. In the center of the back wall, there was a speaker that required headphones to listen to the assortment of music. Below the wall speaker lied a vent, and further to the right was a filthy toilet. The left wall held a steel bunk in possession of a thin, dirty mattress.

Facing the front of the cell, just above the bars, there are two wall to wall shelves. You had to stand on a bunk in order to reach the first shelf and you had to climb the bars if you wanted to reach the second.

After a look around my newly acquired living quarters, I turned off the light and seated myself on the bunk in search of a mental escape via one of the blaring televisions on wall, but little good it did me. Thoughts of the day's earlier events invaded my mind.

"You're hereby sentenced to death..."

Approximately an hour later an officer sat a couple of bags down in front of my cell. "I know you thought I forgot about you," he stated as he began removing the contents from the bags.

"Yes, I did," I replied in an attempt to fill any lingering void.

Upon my arrival at the prison, I was allowed to spend my thirty dollars in the unit's commissary. And now that I had the items, my desire was to smoke a cigarette to calm my nerves. Yes, a cigarette will make a difference. A cigarette will assist me in my focus, I believed, on something positive, only to no avail. The cigarette only assisted me in a slower form of death and a deeper focus into what transpired earlier that day.

"Hey, look out officer," I called as he used a remote control to turn off the televisions. "I need some sheets, and stuff to clean this cell."

"I'll bring you something after I get my count." He replied dryly.

The day had been long and dreadful, and I could feel it taking its toll on my body. I laid on the bunk staring at the ceiling before drifting off to sleep, but in the middle of the night, I found myself awakened by the cold sweeping through the wing. Looking around, I

soon discovered that the officer working the wing had failed to fulfill my request. Disappointed, I placed my arms inside my shirt and balled up into a fetal position to seek warmth.

"Hey man," I heard the husky voice say in my mild sleeping state. I was a bit frightened by how my eyes focused on the black, heavy, set man. I was laying on my back with my head by the bars, so I saw him upside down. I immediately rose to a sitting position on the bunk as my eyes were trying to adjust to the daylight.

"Here you some sheets," he stated as he handed them to me. "It was a few people who told me 'bout you coming in las' night and dey was wonderin' how old you was. Some thought you to be 'bout fifteen or sixteen years old."

"Naw, hey," I said changing the subject, "Is it possible that I could get something to clean this dirty cell with?"

He was responsible for cleaning up the wing. He would primarily sweep and occasionally mop the floor. And even though he wasn't required to do so, he would run errands for those of us locked down. Of course, he would expect compensation.

He returned with cleaning supplies and left without saying anything.

After cleaning up for a while, I attempted to write a letter. But who could I write that would care to hear from me now?

Most people I considered to write's only response would be, "I told you so!" Many predicted my going to prison, but I wonder if the thought ever crossed any of their minds that I would wind up in prison —on death row.

How did I get here? What road did I take that caused me to end up here?

There are many pot holes in the street of life, yet, normally a sign of detour provides direction to safety; a way around, a way out, a way to hurdle every obstacle.

I had never witnessed a sign that warned, "DEATH ROW!'," or did I misread?

Perhaps.

The dancing thoughts of yesterday will reveal...

CHAPTER II

Why?

How often do dreams become nightmares?

My dream became a nightmare as I stood facing *her*, the one woman that had abandoned me fourteen years prior to this day. It was August 4, 1964, that she pushed in agony to allow me passage through the door of her womb.

I believed long ago, that this day of our meeting would turn out to be a day of excitement; a day filled with joy and laughter that would echo throughout the area of our meeting.

"Let's forget yesterday and go from here", was the sentiment I always held in my heart. But here I was, greeted with discontentment. A slap in the face or a beating could have felt better.

Perhaps the escape of a bullet propelled from the chamber of one's gun would have had a better sound then all the voices in question in my head. The most famous of all —why?! What did I do to you to deserve you walking out on me when I was a baby, mama?! For what reason did you not want me, mama?!

Tears I wanted to cry but could not find. What was it that I did wrong, mama?! Was my cry as a baby too loud, mama?! Was I too expensive, mama?! I won't cry no more, mama! I'll be the best son you or any mama could ever want, mama! Mama, please mama!!! Whatever it was that I did, please forgive me! I won't do it no more, mama!

There was no response to surface concerning any of my questions and pleas in my head. We stared at each other like two people at the commencement of a gun fight to see who would make the first move.

My father, who brought me to this dreadful event, stepped forward as though he was trying to prevent things from becoming disarrayed between two gunfighters. I didn't understand what he said as he approached her, but it was obvious that he made her aware of who I was when he pointed at me. Still there was no greeting of any sort or exchange of words between us.

The moment had fallen below discomforting. I felt like an abused child who found refuge in the far dark corner. That little boy I returned to being; abused by neglect, abandonment, and rejection where down the road from them lived physical, verbal, and emotional abuse.

As I had done much in my fourteen years, I wanted to run, run back to the far dark corner of the streets where I found drugs, and alcohol, a place of refuge to escape the bitter abuses that tore away at my soul like a bitter tornado sweeping through a small town, leaving scattered debris to reveal the capacity of its destruction.

Seven years prior to this meeting, I discovered that the woman I had been calling mama was actually my grandmother on my father's side of the family. She also had a daughter, my aunt. In the back of my mind, I always wondered how she could be calling her mama like me without her being my sister.

"Mama," my aunt began after she heard my question. "It's 'bout time we tell 'em."

The shock of her statement pierced my heart before I actually got the chance to hear the story. My eyes darted between my aunt and mama as I braced myself for the impact.

"Boy, sit your butt down. I call her mama because she is my mama. She's your grandmother. When you was a baby, your mama gave you to my mama."

"If your mama was to walk up out there now, I wouldn't know her," my grandmother intervened. "She intended to give you to some other family, but I told her that if she didn't want you, I'll keep and raise you, and you been wit' me ever since."

I discovered that I also had brothers and sisters and it immediately became a dream for me to find them one day.

"We love you, and will always love you," my aunt said as she took me in her arms.

"And I'm still mama!" My Grandmother assured me.

Although I had acquired the dream to one day find my biological mother, and brothers and sisters, the news had adversely affected me. My grades and behavior fell below the norm some time afterward and I found myself on the street of rebellion.

But now, seven years after the discovery, I stood face to face with the one woman who appeared to dread the day that I would walk into her life.

My father and I took a familiar trip from Shreveport, Louisiana to Dallas, Texas. He had been summoned by my aunt, who I was living with in Shreveport to come pick me up from a juvenile facility where I had been on numerous occasions.

At the time of my arrest I was on probation. My aunt would usually come pick me up afterward, but she was fed up with me at this point and told me I wasn't welcome back in her home.

My father was furious upon his arrival, and he made it very clear. I heard him tell a juvenile authority that he was "wiping his hands of me"—he was "quitting" me. But my question was… how could he do this when he'd never had an interest in being there for me to begin with?

 Matter of fact, he walked out on me too. He left me with *his* mother, married a woman that wasn't mine, and then landed himself in prison. Yet, here at this critical stage in my life he expressed the will to walk out on me—as if he had been there before. I'm sure he must have recognized the trauma that was imprisoned in my soul, yet he offered no assistance.

The silence was always deafening us.

We rode all the way from Shreveport to Tyler without saying a word.

There were many things I wish my father would have shared with me. Above all, at this particular stage in my life, it would have been nice if he could've shared *his* prison experiences and run-ins with the law. Maybe, just maybe, that would've prevented me from traveling the same path. I'm sure it was obvious that I was well on my way.

We must ponder the steps we take in life because eventually we'll find someone walking in what we're leaving behind.

The hours of silence on this trip were finally broken when I heard his hushed voice say, "Don't tell your stepmother, alright?"

"Alright..." I replied suspiciously.

I don't know what happened to his first wife, but apparently, after prison he took another.

Although his statement was hushed, it had tremendous impact that came crashing down on me like the collapse of a demolished building.

"Don't tell your stepmother!" Something was unbefitting in this statement. Am I that much of an outcast that it wasn't feasible for me to have a mother?

My stepmother had ten children and they were aware of their father's whereabouts, so what made me different? These questions would remain at the center of my thoughts, never to be answered. And all I could draw from the depths of this well was that famous question...

WHY?

CHAPTER III

DADDY STREET CORNER.

The streets of Dallas offered dreadful memories. I had almost been born in them, and as far as I knew, I had been conceived in them. Perhaps that is why they often found me in them. And upon my trip back to Dallas, they beckoned me to return to them.

It would be feasible to say that although they offered dreadful memories, I adored them, because as soon as the voice of disdain rang out in my father's house, I would run back to them.

They offered a place of refuge. They could cover the scars that had been inflicted upon me. In them I could run! I could hide and in hiding, I could be who I wanted to be. I could be an adult although a minor. I could have a high paying job, yet be unemployed and financially embarrassed. I could have a car, yet possess run over shoes due to excessive walking. I could have a wife, yet not have a woman at all. I could have a child, yet be a virgin. I could own a home, yet live in a cardboard box. I could be a college graduate, yet be a high school drop out. I could be a chef, yet not know how to cook. But there's a place in hiding where the one doing so will find that they are only hiding from themselves. Simply because they are afraid to be who they see themselves becoming, or ashamed of being who they've turned out to be. And I was well on my way to hiding —hiding from myself!

As always, my three stepbrothers would greet me with excitement. From experience, I knew it would not last long.

The scene was always set and everyone would do their part while the lights and cameras were on and the audience was watching, but as soon as the lights were out, the camera was off and the audience was not watching, they would step out of their acting roles and be who they really were —my enemies. I had too many enemies already without them and was quickly becoming my own worst enemy.

On numerous occasions I had to fight them. I lived with them for the first time when I was about eight, around the time my father got out of prison. I recall making the mistake of fighting one of them. I guess he felt humiliated at his loss, because our fist fight would soon turn into a knife fight. He chased me with a butcher's knife, through the house, around the front yard, the backyard, down the street— I ran until I couldn't run no more. I had always enjoyed running, racing to the finish line, but here was a matter where I was running for my life and it wasn't enjoyable.

I don't remember what settled the matter, but I do remember thinking that should we ever fight again, I was definitely going to use a weapon on him before he used one on me.

They enjoyed seeing pain inflicted upon me. Once we all got into something, knocking on different neighbors' doors and running before they answered. They told their mother that I was responsible for what we were doing. She then told my father and without question, he stormed into the room where I was and began beating me. The only support they offered was their laughter.

I had determined that things would be different this time. My feet were aching for the pavement of the streets and sure enough, I would return to them in two months.

My step family seemed to complain and gripe about every little thing I did.

"I ain't got time to be tripping with these folks," I told myself.

But deep within I was looking for an excuse to get away from them. An excuse to answer the call of the streets. They welcomed me, they enjoyed me, and without realizing it, they were dragging me in the depths of despair. They held me, they hid me, but they had no protection for me. And what I needed the most was protection from myself.

The stone-throwing of my step family's abusive words and behavior forced me out into the dark, dreary, and cold night with fear as my constant companion, as I hid in the shadows of the streets for the first time.

It all became unbearable as I pursued the attention of my father who showed no concern for me. I endured all I could stand from my step family. It was merely a matter of existence without concern.

No longer would I merely exist. The streets had a place for me and concern about me. It was time to get to know a new daddy.

Daddy Street Corner was his name and many children he adopted who experienced the same. He is the daddy that adopts the bruised, battered and beaten. The rejected, abused and destitute. He has played doctor to many minor daughters who pushed out their children to him behind dumpsters. He embraces little boys and little girls who are on the run from the clutches of Mr. Lust. He has witnessed men and women stagger to their death. Many of his sons and daughters sell their bodies for money or just a hit of dope. He has witnessed many rapes, robberies and riots. He has witnessed the death of many dope fiends overdosing in the stench of alleys. He has experienced oozing blood soaking into him from bodies plundered to their death in suicide; gunshot, and knife wounds. He refereed many fist fights turned fatal.

No one he adopted has ever went homeless, even if the home was just a cardboard box. No one has ever gone broke, for he will make a way to lure a robbery victim into a danger zone. No one has ever been unemployed, for there is always the job of theft and robbery. No one has ever been without transportation, for he would always direct his children to unprotected vehicles. No one has ever been without a mate, for there was always a prostitute, homosexual, or unsatisfied housewife seeking companionship. No one has ever been without food to eat, for he served breakfast from a trashcan and lunch and dinner from a dumpster to the fill.

He cuddles, cradles and cares for the desolate, deranged and doomed. He breeds prostitutes, homosexuals, rapists, dope fiends, gamblers, murderers, pimps, players and pushers.

Daddy Street Corner has raped, robbed, killed, and even destroyed. He has raped many of their dignity, robbed many of their time, killed many dreams, and destroyed many lives.

In him lives no prejudice, for he accepts all, no matter what race, breed, color, or cultural background; no matter what age, shape, size, or style.

And I, at the tender age of 9, was a new face in the family; running from danger to destruction.

The downtown streets of Dallas found me in search of a car to steal. Apparently, I hadn't learned my lesson. This was the very reason my father had to come get me out of Louisiana. Still I hadn't had enough.

I don't recall exactly where or when I met this guy, but as I was walking through downtown Dallas, I heard his voice calling,

"Terry…Terry!"

That was my street alias. Up until then I had forgotten about that name and this caused him to have to say it a number of times before I reacted to it.

"Yea," I said as he approached me.

"What you up to?"

"Nothin' much," I lied.

"I got my car parked up the street. Won't we go get a bite to eat and go over to my place?" he offered.

"Ah'ight." I shrugged.

The downtown streets of Dallas were infested with its share of men like him, an open homosexual, who cruised the dark streets of Dallas in search of young boys and men to proposition for sex.

We rode through the dark Dallas streets with loud music blaring as the summer night's air breezed through the Grand Toronado.

Little did he know…

I would not be going home with him.

CHAPTER IV

COUNTRY DRUNK.

I had to leave Shreveport with my father after my run-in with the Shreveport law officials.

Now I was leaving my father in Dallas after problems with the Dallas law officials.

I had stolen the guy's car who was trying to "take me to his place."

He left his keys in the ignition when he went to get our food, and when he returned, I was gone.

Shreveport law officials expunged my probation period for car theft due to my father's agreement to take me to Dallas, but they didn't stipulate a time period concerning my return, so about two-and a half months later, I returned to Shreveport…7 months before my 1 year probation period would have been up.

During this time, my grandmother was working at a nursing home in Dallas providing twenty-four-hour care for her rich patient. She paid for my bus fare to return to Shreveport.

My aunt had forgiven me for stealing her car and accepted me back into her home.

My grandmother would come home for about a week in between 2 month work periods.

At some point of my stay in Dallas, I told my aunt and grandmother of my mother's whereabouts, through separate telephone conversations. They immediately expressed their desire to meet her.

Face to face I found myself once again with the woman who had given birth to me.

I could not understand what was happening, as on this occasion her attitude had changed. Perhaps she suffered from a personality disorder. Perhaps the excitement of meeting my aunt and grandmother caused her attitude to change. Perhaps she needed to hear that I was willing to forgive her. Then I began to wonder as I looked back at the time we first met. Perhaps the timing was just wrong.

During our first meeting, she had walked into the restaurant of the truck-stop where my father and I were sharing a cold drink; with a man she seemed to be dating and didn't say two words to me.

Whatever the reason, I was willing to look beyond the first occurrence.

Although I desired answers as to why she walked out on me, I still wanted to get to know the woman who gave birth to me that summer's night in '64.

I stood in the background of the excitement as I had done in tine shadows of the streets to observe what transpired. Immediately after my aunt and grandmother finished hugging everyone, I approached my mother for an embrace. My nerves were on edge as I feared being rejected by her again. I was in unfamiliar territory, where I knew no one. There were no city street corners to run to, so I would have to stand my ground in the event that rejection slapped me in the face again.

"My son," I knew were the words escaping her lips, or perhaps it was merely my imagination standing at the door of my ears that caused me to hear the words I so longed to hear from her; along with "I love you!"

My father brought me to this residence in search of my mother, before we arrived at the truck stop on our way to Dallas. I had met my little brother and sister, and my Mama's mother. They revealed so much more excitement at our second meeting.

My little sister, who looked to be about 8, approached my mother as I was walking away. "Mama, why did you give Toby away?" she asked in pursuit of cutting away at the hidden truth.

My mother immediately dropped her head... No response.

I found out I wasn't the only one she abandoned.

I wondered if she would ever answer the question of her curious daughter, or reveal to us the dark trap door secrets she was in possession of, concerning the majority of her children.

Country living was nothing new to me. My first experience occurred when I was approximately 4 or 5 years old, My grandmother and I moved from Dallas to Bethany, Texas to live with my aunt and her husband who lived on a small farm with cows, chickens, and roosters.

It was interesting to see how my aunt and uncle would milk a cow, or chop off the neck of a chicken; pluck, clean, cook and serve it for dinner.

Because there was no bathroom in the house, we were required to use an outhouse and take baths in a foot tub. There was also a well we drew water from.

Now I was to return to country living.

My mother had moved into another part of Tyler with a man by the name of Ivan Phillip about a month after our second meeting. In pursuit of establishing a mother-son relationship, I moved in with them. I thought he would object to my living in his home, but he said nothing. As a matter of fact, he welcomed me.

Ivan was about forty-two or forty-three years old. He had to walk with a cane due to a lame leg. He worked as a tractor driver, cutting hay and he invited me to work with him. The most I was required to do was drive either his tractor or car to a location from the tractor shed to a job site.

My little brother and I would usually ride in the cab of the cool tractor with him as he cut hay. He enjoyed country music blaring from the radio mounted in the tractor's cab.

Ivan was a man of very few words. And when he spoke, one would have to strain to hear him; that is until one night he came home drunk. I had been living there for about a month when this occurred. I had never witnessed him displaying such offensive behavior.

In the living room of his house we sat in wonder concerning Ivan because he was usually home in bed at this hour. I was approximately fourteen. Seated were: my mother, my little brother and sister, Ivan's sister, her little boy, the man from next door, and myself.

Ivan walked in country drunk. His cussing erupted in the house with volcanic thunder. I was surprised, yet entertained by his behavior. He kneeled before my mother with the appearance of a man proposing.

"Every day I come in from work, there's nothing cooked and dem' same dirty ass dishes is in there from last week. I'm tired of comin' home from work to provide for you and yo' chirren and I ain't got shit to eat or a dish to eat it out of!"

"If you trying to tell me ta leave, then I'll go!" my mother snapped back.

"I'm not telling you ta leave, I'm telling you, you can't stay in this fuckin' house all day and not do a damn thing!" he shouted,

"I go out and pay these fuckin' bills to keep a roof over y'all head, and I got nothin' in return coming. I'm sick ah this shit!" Ivan struggled to stand to his feet. Once he found some balance, he started motioning with his hand as though he was going to hit her.

The knock of violence pounded my thoughts at Ivan's gestures towards my mother, and the opportunity to reveal to her that I would protect her stood center stage.

I had previously sought the whereabouts of weapons in the house. My curiosity led me to discover 2 guns. Ivan was in possession of a .22 rifle and .410 shotgun. Therefore, I was a step ahead of my panic-stricken mother's request.

"Toby!" my mother called when Ivan was distracted. Go and get rid of those guns in the closet!"

After I retrieved the guns from the closet, I threw them out of their bedroom window.

Upon my return, Ivan reverted to cussing her again. I stormed pass them going outside to retrieve the guns.

I moved the .410 to a different location and checked the .22 for proper loading.

Flashbacks of moments surfaced from my memory bank. I had witnessed young boys in discussion about their mothers. There was never an unkind word, never a disrespectful moment in their description of their mothers. There was always the expression of love and desire to protect mama.

I would experience shame, and struggle to prevent the tears in the wells of my eyes from streaming down my face to hear such expression of love concerning their mamas!

Their expression of love for their mothers would cut me like a knife. I longed for a mother, the woman that carried me for 9 months, the one who experienced sickness because of me, the one who experienced pain in the late hours of the night, the one who pushed in pain to give me birth, one who was overcome with joy the night it was said a man-child was born.

There were no little boy cuts and bruises to take to mama to nurse, no silly kid questions, no hard math problems, no questions about the little girls who would one day pique my interest; because mama was non-existent in my life.

Although this chapter of the book was missing from my life, there was another chapter to emerge. A chapter that would open to a series of hooks with pages unfolding in mystery to provide great interest, only to wind up in disappointment and provide discouragement to its reader. A chapter that found a "grown-boy" in possession of an instrument of death.

An instrument that has wounded and killed many men, women, boys, and girls found in the hands of rage. Rage that not merely erupted from present occurrences, but dangerously erupted from past occurrences that presently tormented the soul of its victim. The victim who stood in the shadow of country darkness in possession of a deadly aim, and desire to protect the one that introduced him to shame, struggle and hurt.

My voice disturbed the calm of the night as I called out to the man proposing harm to my mother… to face harm.

His steps displayed his drunken state of being. I observed as he approached the door.

The smell of death was in the night air. The radar of the situation revealed astounding percentages of the horrific possibilities — a fallen victim.

Could my mother now see me as a son she loved? The son she wished somewhere in the depths of her heart that she didn't walk out on?

I didn't recognize it at the time, but any of us could have been seriously or fatally injured.

 The percentage of injuries and deaths that occur through a ricocheting bullet or misfiring .22 handgun or rifle are staggering.

The visiting neighbor immediately emerged to prevent Ivan's harm as he put his own life in jeopardy when he speedily approached me. Although my finger was on the trigger, the neighbor hit the gun upward with a marital art type block and I allowed him to take it without resistance.

In order to remove me out of the environment, the neighbor convinced me to get in his car.

The neighborhood club he took me to displayed its open sign of business with blaring music that would render disturbance to any stillness of the night, and lure any uninterested person into its intoxicating grips. My desire for violence quickly subsided when I commenced to getting the intoxicants in my system.

When my eyes opened, it was around mid-morning. I had laid down in Ivan's house at approximately 2 or 3AM fully dressed in the event that I would have to get up fighting or running, but the liquor and marijuana I had at the neighborhood club acted as a sedative.

My little brother made me aware of Ivan's early morning departure and the fact that he didn't think he remembered me threatening him with his gun.

I had been discouraged to learn that my mother and Ivan were in the bed together when I came in during the middle of the night.

As I faced her during the later morning hours, she said nothing, and the look on her face was expressionless. I assumed that she was more displeased with me then pleased.

In the country, one can be drunk without concern of being arrested for public intoxication. They can holler, shout, and scream without concern of any neighbors calling the cops for creating a disturbance.

There are no stop signs or traffic lights and no concern for any radar detection for speeding. The worst there is to run into is a tree.

As I sat on the porch of Ivan's house, he drove up in a freshly wrecked car.

"Hey, come here, Toby and get this drink outta my car," Ivan shouted as he struggled to get out of his car. It was obvious that he had already begun the party as he stumbled toward me.

"Come on and have you a drink there boy," Ivan said after I sat the fifth of gin and six pack of Coors next to him on the porch.

"Let the party begin," I said to myself after taking a drink of gin and chasing it with the beer.

We sat on the porch drinking like 2 old winos who'd gotten together to get drunk and share war stories.

"What happened to your car?" I asked.

"I ran into a ditch and flipped it. Had to get a wrecker to help me get it out."

There was no use in going into detail about it because it was very obvious that he was in no condition to drive. Surprisingly he made it back in one piece.

I discovered from him that after the death of his father, he vowed to never drink again. I had no idea that he was a recovering alcoholic, but there he sat on the porch experiencing relapse in the rehab of his life. Relapse that occurred after he met my mother.

CHAPTER V

BRICK LAYER

I enjoyed Ivan's entertainment when he was
under the influence of alcohol. He would sit
and nod and fall out in the middle of the floor
after a slurred conversation no one could
understand. He could lie out on the floor for
hours leaving us to have to walk over him. It
seemed that the only thing that would cause
him to stir is when I or my little brother would
try to take his money out of his shirt pocket
where he would usually keep it. Even though
he had quit working, he continued to keep
plenty of money.

Often, he would pay for me to do things. On
one particular occasion, he gave me 5 dollars
just to throw a couple of tires into a fire. He
would keep the gas tank in his car full and
allow me to drive it. I especially enjoyed the
fact that he would keep liquor around. The

party would begin in the morning and wouldn't end until the evening.

Everything was okay until one day, he grabbed my little brother who was playing with him as he laid on the couch in his normal drunken state. He wrestled my little brother down onto the floor like he was a man. He was only eleven years old at the time.

"What the fuck you think you doing?! Let my fuckin' brother go!"

I demanded as I struggled to get my little brother from under his death grip. I held him by his neck, punched him in his back and in the back of his head but he still wouldn't release him. I grabbed him under his arm pits applying as much pressure as I could. As I held him, my little brother was squirming his way free of the hold Ivan had on him. As I continued to cuss him, I kneed him in the back until my little brother worked his way out of his grasp. When he was only held by his leg by Ivan, I ran out of the house and found a brick.

My little brother was still trying to pull away from him upon my return. I cocked the brick back as far as I could as I stood on the outside of the house. Just as my little brother stumbled his way toward me and the screen door was closing, I threw the brick as hard as I could. The brick tore through the screen from the force, hitting Ivan on the right side of his face, causing blood to pour from the opened wound.

The misery within me stirred enough to finally draw blood. For a moment I found myself thinking as Ivan squirmed and screamed in pain,

"I'll kill you !"

For a moment, time seemed to have stood still as I stood over Ivan and watched him wallow in his blood. The possibility of becoming a fourteen year old murderer beckoned. There was nothing to accomplish in my future. Trouble was the house I often hung around in. Trouble was quickly becoming my home.

When my rage had subsided, I began to think of my mother.

Oh, my mother... She would be terribly disturbed. This was her bread and butter lying on the edge of death.

Upon me and my little brother's arrival to where my mother was visiting neighbors, he made her aware of what happened as I instructed him to do. There were about 10-15 people in the house, and all of them went to Ivan's rescue.

I found myself seated on the porch of the neighbor's house, wondering what lay ahead for the both of us. But I was primarily concerned for myself.

Ivan's face was stitched. The scar was about 5 to 6 inches long down the right side of his face.

As 2 drunks would do, as soon as he got away from the hospital, we began our drinking together again as though nothing happened, and I continued to live under his roof.

Somehow my aunt received the news of all that was taking place during my stay in Tyler, TX which prompted her to come and get me. She expressed concern as to how my mother could allow me to live under such conditions.

Apparently, it was of no concern between Ivan and I.

The one thing my aunt never knew was that Ivan and I became the best of drinking buddies. We could half kill each other one day and continue to be the best of drunken friends the next.

Disappointment was my constant companion. It greeted me once more at the discovery that I would be leaving Tyler.

I had a job offer from Ivan's employer. I was merely required to count bales of hay the employees delivered to the barn during the day. My method of payment had not been determined, but the employer was popular for having satisfied employees even if it meant overpaying them. But this would end up on my list of would-have-been's due to the disruption of Mr. Disappointment, who also disrupted my opportunities to hang onto the coat of my intoxicated supplier of intoxicants.

He would now merely be a memory. I would remember his kindness but often in life, the memory of the negatives overpowered those of kindness, although more kindness than negativity was exemplified.

Somehow we desire others to see all the good in us when in fact, more bad is displayed every day.

Even though I would remember Ivan's kindness in allowing me to live under his roof, I would allow the negativity to step out of the home of my thoughts to reveal to others the outweighing memory I had of his unkind

gesture towards my mother. Even though I
would remember Ivan's kindness in allowing
me to eat from his table, I would prepare the
meal for others to taste of the memory of his
unkind behavior toward my little brother.
Above all, I would invite into the living room
of my mind, others to partake of the memory
of the many intoxicated moments we shared.

CHAPTER VI

EDUCATIONAL SICKNESS.

Life possesses many schools, and the most prestigious school I attended taught: robbery 101, prostitution 505, and murder 187.

If anyone desires enrollment, there's an instructor available for any subject. If there is a desire to learn the technique in selling dope, of learning the art of thievery, of learning the language of lies, of learning the drama of abuse of any kind, of learning the steps of cheating, there is an instructor available for each course.

Those who can't read or have the desire to read experience the joys of not being required to read or study from any book. There are no tests to prepare for and no report cards to take home.

Although these instructors never sleep, and never rest, they are never exhausted, and they never complain. Although they experience the failure of many students who turn to an honest way of living, many have graduated and there is an alarming rate of those scheduled to graduate.

I was always at the top of my class, making my instructors very proud of me, yet failing to fully comprehend the magnitude of the requirements for graduation. The better one becomes at what they're majoring in, the more one desires to achieve, and the more one achieves, the more careless they become. In this form of study, carelessness leads to graduating with honors.

The school that would teach me about work ethics, about honest survival, I had no interest in. I dreaded getting up early in the morning to attend school where there existed rules to abide by, certain classes to be in at a specified time, books, tests, and report cards.

Educational sickness struck me especially hard in the sixth grade. I had begun to run a behavior disorder fever that forced me into the intensive care of the system causing the school officials to provide me with constant monitoring.

For the first time of my going to school, at Hillsdale Elementary in Shreveport, we were required to stay in one class all day. I was suffocating. We were allowed a couple of recess periods which were the only periods I would look forward to. I was too active to remain in one place all day. My deteriorated behavior and being active kept me in trouble, along with the boiling over of the traumas of the past.

When the alarm of my behavioral disorder sounded, the school officials would contact my aunt like the doctors of a medical facility that contacted the next of kin when the patient progressed to an extremely critical stage. On many occasions she would come to the school as though she was coming to my rescue. I would get suspended or the school would give me the day off due to the eruption of my flawed behavior—fighting, class disruption, and getting caught touching the girls. This school required some excitement, and who of all people could provide the excitement it needed but me?

The teacher didn't help much with her strict rules. I always thought of the elderly Caucasian woman to be mean and racist. She would give me a hard time. I didn't realize it at the time, but she was going out of her way to help me, but I couldn't see it due to my behavioral disorders.

Although many find school a bore, it is of importance to pursue some form of education. Because of a lack of education, the intelligent trash man failed to become the executive he was capable of being. Because of a lack of education, the intelligent ditch digger failed to become the doctor that he was capable of being. Because of a lack of education, the intelligent woman failed to become the news reporter she was capable of being. The lack of an education has sent many into the trenches of war for the purpose of surviving.

Many have succumbed to educational sickness because of their desires to pursue that which has no value, no substance, which leads to a dead-end street, the street I had once decided to travel.

Education, I'm sure, would have been important to me if it was not available for me.

For many African Americans, education was not available and this was somehow an incentive for them to pursue education, but for me, it was unimportant, I was uninterested. I had determined that there was nothing to life and there was nothing for me to get out of life. Therefore, what could education provide me that I was not already capable of obtaining?

Drugs, sex, alcohol— the material things of life that have drawn many into the abyss of destruction.

Upon my entry into junior high I started occasional class skipping. I found excitement in walking the corridors of the school under the influence of alcohol and marijuana; ducking and dodging into the restrooms for the purpose of hiding and for smoking cigarettes and weed, being a distraction to others who were in class in pursuit of obtaining some form of education that the school system had to offer.

I had looked forward to attending school in Tyler, but my and Ivan's drunken behavior prevented that.

Being the "new kid on the block" drew attention in my direction with the young girls. I was lacking in conversation, so I tried to use my appearance to compensate for that. But as the sporting fisherman does, I was required to throw back into the sea that which I couldn't keep after their discovery of my lack of conversation.

My conversation was different when under the influence of alcohol. Although I rarely had anything to say, the alcohol had plenty to say, and I was always willing to be its mouthpiece, but I couldn't afford to stay drunk all the time.

Upon my return to Shreveport, LA from Tyler, TX, I entered into my sophomore year of high school at Huntington High. Although I was in my sophomore year, I was still at the freshman level due to my failing the previous year.

I had been in and out of so many schools, I've lost track of some of them!

After I got kicked out of Huntington for reasons I don't recall, I had to go to a school in Shreveport for troubled teenagers known as the school away from school. This was the school I quickly got used to. There were no certain classes to attend and although we all were required to stay in one area all day, there was never a boring moment for me.

My interest to ease any burden of boredom held me captivated in the warm embrace of her delectable smile each time she watched me approach. She possessed a graceful way in expressing herself that drew a response from me which would always allow us to share in a meaningful conversation. We could discuss the weather and I would feel excitement.

It was always a delight to behold her beauty, to have the opportunity to stare in her eyes, to take her into my arms for a sweet embrace. I had a desire for our relationship to blossom and bloom, but it barely took root due to my love of money.

CHAPTER VII

THE LOVE OF MONEY.

The lessons I'd learned about standing in the dark shadows of the night manifested as I observed my prey like a hungry lion in pursuit of the best opportunity to nab its victim. My prey had what I wanted, and I was there to feed on my catch because I was starving. I crept upon him like a lion creeping upon a gazelle.

Although I was no lion, I had something equivalent to a lions' roar that would get the attention of my prey and instill fear in his heart. In order that he knew I came for serious business, I fired a round from the' .22 revolver that echoed under the shed of the gas station into the night like a small explosion. Surprisingly, he took off running, but I couldn't let him get away, he was in possession of what I came for. Although I was no dope-fiend, I wanted money. Even though I had no family to support, I possessed a love for money and I was in deadly pursuit of it!

Money, one needs it as a means of survival, but there's an evil associated with the love of it. For the love of money, men and women have sold their bodies. Many have gambled for it, lied and cheated for it. Many have stolen it from their parents. And for the love of it, I was on the very verge of killing for it.

There was no regard for him or any of his family and friends grieving. The only regard I had was for getting away with his money!

I had come walking but I was planning on leaving riding in "my" new car with "my" easily earned money. That was my attitude, but it didn't turn out that way. The man ran around the gas station building, causing me to run in order to get to him. When I had a clear shot at him, I fired a second time and ran towards him.

"Where's the keys to your car?!"

I demanded as I approached the body lying on the ground. I realized after the question that he had dropped them when he took off running.

50

"I don't have them." He managed to spit out.

"Give me the money! Where's the money?" I said growing impatient.

"I don't have none."

At this point he could have told me anything because my thoughts were distorted. It wasn't supposed to be like this. He disrupted my plans and because of it, he was going to have to suffer the consequence…

Death.

Besides, if he stayed alive, he could identify me.

It had become apparent that I wasn't going to leave with all I came to get. Due to the disruption, the possibility of me leaving period were slim.

Listening had never been top priority on my list, and I would soon pay for my failure to do so.

My aunt had invited me into her room one night to watch a portion of the news. The report revealed a robbery that resulted in a fatality and gunshot injury and the apprehension of two of three suspects. One suspect had been fatally shot by police and a

51

policeman had been shot in the process as I recall. This had occurred at the same gas station I was in the process of robbing.

My aunt had explained how such a fatality could happen to me under the same circumstances.

To me, this was a challenge.

They didn't know what they were doing! I could pull a robbery successfully, leaving the news to report that the suspect got away with an undisclosed amount of money. I had purchased my first gun, a .22 revolver, at the age of fifteen, with a determination to shoot something or somebody. Realizing the danger of a .22 pistol, I had no desire to purchase one, but it was the only thing available for the 12 dollars I had to spend.

The premeditation of my robbery plan ran smoothly but by the day of the robbery I experienced the crooks and turns in the road.

I had walked about two miles from my aunt's house to the place on my robbery list. I had stood around trying to look inconspicuous as I observed my victim and traffic. My nerves were on edge! The right moment never manifested, so I left, hoping that the next night would be more successful, but that was not the case as I stood over the victim who was sitting on the ground pleading for his life.

To me life meant nothing. I hated what life had brought me thus far and was willing to offer it back. My only route, I realized, was through death. Life meant nothing; death was all I wanted. There was no concern when I came into the world, therefore, I could leave quietly without anyone being concerned about my departure. I was often frightened by the thought that I would perhaps be unsuccessful and left to live with a failed suicide attempt.

Since life meant nothing to me, taking life from someone else meant nothing either. I pointed the gun toward his face and shot again. Should there be one to point me out in a court of law, if apprehension was my future, it wouldn't be him, I thought. I discovered after my arrest that I was unsuccessful in committing a homicide. It occurred to me that I had failed to compensate for the kick of the gun. The only bullet wound he suffered hit him in the elbow which occurred as he was running from me.

My arrest had occurred after my traffic light stop. My intentions were to purchase liquor before getting on the interstate to Dallas, Texas.

But I noticed that the police officer on the opposite side of the street looked in my direction with astonishment on his face, with the excitement of a kid in a candy store.

I pulled off slowly watching the rearview mirror, hoping to not draw any more attention then I already had, but it was too late. Surrender and death were my only real options, but I made running a third. An unmarked police vehicle drove closely behind me after I took a back street leading to many businesses near the interstate.

I enjoyed driving fast and reckless. The car I was driving, a Z-28, could reach 100 miles per hour within 8-12 seconds as I had found out during my famous test drive.

Complications intervened. It seemed as though the cops were already parked in the area when I made a turn onto a dead end street. When I stopped the car, cop cars came out of different directions and surrounded the Z-28. As I surrendered, I witnessed many weapons drawn and pointed at me.

My chance to embrace death had arrived, but the voice of my aunt who would constantly tell me about being gunned down by the cops, how it would practically destroy them to make

54

such discovery concerning me, resonated in
my heart to prevent such an embrace.

CHAPTER VIII

END OF MY FIRST LIFE

Although the media was not permitted to mention my name during their report of the crime since I was only 15, one of the employees of the facility I was taken to for my incarceration told me that she, in fact, anticipated me being the actual perpetrator of the reported crime. The question that lingers is: how could she anticipate this when I had never been incarcerated there or anywhere else for any kind of violent behavior? Could the wretched screams I possessed within have somehow escaped my lips on one of the occasions I was around her to alert her that I was capable of committing such violence?

I had been in and out of this facility on many occasions for stealing my aunts' cars and running away from home. Each time my aunt would forgive me and persuade the authorities to release me into her custody, except for the time my father was summoned, but there was no releasing me into her custody after this crime. Trouble had now become my home.

I could no longer go into the kitchen of my aunt's home or anyone else's home to prepare a meal or snack. There were no trips to the store to purchase anything, or in my case, steal anything. I could not call or visit friends. And as for my girlfriend, perhaps someone else would be holding her before my return to freedom's light. The choice I made one winter's night resulted in unwarranted change.

I had never considered the benefits of freedom during my occasional visits to the juvenile facility. They were unimportant to me until I could no longer experience them. I had finally backed myself into a corner in order to obtain something else. Something someone else had worked hard for.

The manifestation of this robbery took place on that night, but the crime occurred long before then. It began when I became impregnated with the thought of devising a plan for the purpose of capitalizing off someone else's' earnings. I refused to put the legs of my thoughts in the stirrups for an abortion.

Instead, I gave birth to them. And as a result, I had to kiss my freedom goodbye and attempt to hold on to what sanity I had left.

I pleaded guilty, in hopes of receiving a shorter sentence… but the judge extended no mercy.

The gavel of justice had sentenced me to juvenile life for armed robbery and attempted murder.

I was fifteen at the time of the crime. My sentence meant that I was required to remain in the boy's home for the rest of my juvenile life —until I was 21.

My court appointed attorney assured me that I would only spend six months in the boys' home as long as I maintained a clean record… but I was more accustomed to doing dirt.

I found a familiar face in the prison dorms. A young man who went by Cadillac, a nickname acquired from being overweight. We met before in the juvenile facility in Shreveport. Now that we were doing time, he would provide me with the rules of incarceration from a prison mentality.

"Look, man," Cadillac began after offering me a seat. "This area here is 'Port City's (Shreveport) area. Dem cats over dhere is New Orl'ans, and over to the middle dhere is where Monroe and Baton Rouge hang out." He nodded his head toward each area he revealed. "And over dhere is the country boys." (guys from various small towns).

The dayroom was spacious with about nine or ten tables. There was a desk at the end for the two officers they called "house parents." On the other side of the building was an area for our lockers and shower and bathroom area. Our beds were upstairs.

I had stepped into a modern day form of segregation. There were specific shower heads, sinks, lockers, and sleeping quarters assigned to specific groups.

Although I would complain, I had no real right, because I was suffering the consequences for the decision I made for the love of money.

We all were too young and inexperienced to realize and understand the magnitude of what our forefathers experienced at the violent hand of racial segregation. Perhaps our ignorance motivated us into participating in such stupidity. Or perhaps there were other contributing factors stemming from how and where we were raised.

At the traumatizing hand of racial segregation, men and women lost their lives, were framed and sent to prison because of being in a place forbidden to their race. Our segregation was simply by choice and had nothing to do with race. Although there were a few Caucasians, the majority of us were African Americans. Our segregation existed merely because of location. And just as the dangers in racial segregation existed, the dangers of being in the wrong place in the boys' home existed.

Fighting would be the primary result, but gang violence and death were also common outcomes.

The time had started to drag. Boredom began to settle in. Fear shoved it's way in one night when I was met by a flurry of punches that left me with a bloody nose, shattered pride, and disturbing laughter to make its acquaintance; even from Cadillac.

Fighting had always been one of my enjoyments, especially when I knew I had a win, but this was different. A win could cause me hospitalization. At this point, I arrived in the ring of fight night to realize that I really didn't know how to fight. I had been fighting young boys I believed had much less experience than me. If it appeared as though they had more experience in the middle of the fight, I believed they could not out-run me. Running had become my favorite sport of participation. It was practically my way of life. If I couldn't run from something physically, I would run mentally, primarily to the sea of intoxicants to drown my problems. But as I stood with blood pouring from my face and my pride shattered in pieces for all the spectators to trample on, I had nowhere to run physically or mentally. Oh yes, I could run back to the many prior fights, but I could not conjure anything from them because of entering the reality of the matter…

I didn't know how to fight.

Freedom's light provided much room for running. If running wasn't the desire or way out, there was always a gun or some form of weaponry, but I had nothing to get my hands on in this case. I would definitely need a gun. The guy was from New Orleans and I learned that they operate as a gang. My small frame couldn't handle all those kicks and punches, but if I allowed this episode to end here I would have more than punches and kicks to worry about.

We're only allowed one opportunity to make a first impression. The impression I left would cause many to view me as a weak coward, and this would motivate many to pursue turning me into their girlfriend. Well, I wouldn't be able to lay right. Running would become my only option.

CHAPTER IX.

RUNNING STILL.

Although there were no fences on the yard, men riding motorcycles were responsible for outside security.

Approximately two days after my fight night, I decided that I would make a run for it, in order to find a way to re-group. My thoughts were cloudy and the storm of me being somebody's girlfriend was raging. An umbrella would do no good, I needed shelter.

My request to my counselor to move out of the dorm went on deaf ears, forcing me to make my own move.

I devised no complicated plans as to how I would seek shelter from the raging storm headed into my life, but this particular morning would be unusually busy. Security would get a considerable amount of time to operate their radios and ride their bikes at frightening speed.

Everyone appeared to be in a robotic state as they marched down stairs during our usual morning ritual that began at 0600 hours.

This particular morning belonged to me. I would be the star attraction. I would have no limousine to ride in the back of, but I would be on the move. There would be no people gathered to request my autograph, but there would be people gathered to devise a strategy to locate my whereabouts. I would have no center stage performance, yet I would be the center of attention. I would not get the opportunity to be on the cover of a magazine, yet I would be exposed on the open cover of my criminal file. No one would seek from me a story about my life, yet the story of my criminal life would lie exposed for all who were interested.

Although no one was running on my heels, I was on the run. Although my legs weren't in motion, I was on the run. Although I wasn't ducking and dodging behind buildings, I was on the run.

Running had become so much a part of me that I could run physically without setting my feet in motion at rapid speed.

My running alerted security, I noticed, as I could hear the blaring of their radios and the speeding of their motorcycles. Their actions revealed that I was far, but I was close. Their actions revealed that I had made it beyond the compound, but I never left the building. Under the bed I lay still on the floor for approximately fifteen to twenty minutes before one of the house parents returned to find me.

Everyone thought that I had fallen asleep under the bed. Usually someone would wake the guy who fell asleep, but no one had tried to get my attention so I could be included in the morning count, which I intended to be excluded from.

I don't recall exactly who I spoke with afterward, but I do remember informing someone that my incident was purposed to get me moved from that particular dorm. Mission accomplished!

The location I was moved to wasn't as intense as where I moved from, but there were interesting moments.

My primary interests were the nights the house parents would allow us to "take-five".. (fight).

A take-five was when we were allowed to call out someone to the middle of the floor for the purpose of getting something off of our chest. However, I quickly lost interest on the night that I had been chosen to fight.

My character had already been marred by failing to fight previously. I had no desire for this but to not go would be fatal. I eased my marred character, pride, and fear off the top bunk of the bed. The walk to the middle of the floor was excruciating. Deep within I was hoping the house parent would call it off or the guy would change his mind. Neither happened.

There was no announcement as to when we were to begin or how we were to fight. The commencement of a couple of his punches hit their mark. Fight time! In my face they came fast. Damn, I forgot to duck… or was I supposed to throw my hands up? My thinking was distorted, even before my arrival in the middle of the floor. Instead of considering how to properly formulate a punch or protect myself, I was busy trying to formulate a voice in my head that would be loud enough for everyone to hear, especially me, that this fight was called off, but such voices were non-existent. The only voice I got to hear were the voices of those punches making their connection up side my head.

I threw a few punches, I think I got one to land somewhere. I might have hit myself, I couldn't tell because I was swinging with my head down. I attempted to take him to a wrestling match, but he wouldn't join me. He would push off to return to throwing his punches. Finally, after what seemed like about thirty minutes, I heard the voice I so longed for, the voice that announced, "that's it!"

I climbed in my bunk with fresh knots upside my head to accompany me.

"I hadn't done anything to this guy to cause him to want to fight me. Why's he tripping wit' me?" I questioned to myself.

Each night that we were allowed to take-five, he would call me out and each night I would desire to hear that voice I so longed for, but I would always hear the voice of those connecting punches upside my head.

After a while, I started to get better. I guess my fighting improved, he stopped calling me out after about the seventh time.

Although he constantly called me out, he never sought to bully me. I could only guess that he was providing me with experience. He too was from Shreveport, and had previously experienced incarcerations' battles.

The next time I had a fight was a shocking experience.

The gym was full of people, but there were only about six of us playing basketball. It was obvious, this guy was trying to bully me. Well, I had enough of anyone trying to take something from me, and putting up with somebody's mess. All of a sudden, after he had been talking trash to me, he threw his hands up. Toe to toe we stood fighting. May the best man win. I had found confidence in my fighting and this confidence caused him to land on the floor dazed. I don't know what I hit him with or how I hit him to cause him to greet the gym's floor with his behind, but I knew that I needed to cultivate it for the future.

Although the fight I failed to fight would linger over my head, the fact that I would fight took precedence. I never experienced problems again.

CHAPTER X

CORRUPTED BEHAVIOR.

On a silver platter I had been served the hopes and dreams of an early release, but disappointment spoiled my appetite when I discovered that I had been served a raw meal.

The serving of my attorney's appetizing words heightened my taste buds for this special day of my return to freedom's light, all to end up in the garbage can for disposal.

Although I wasn't allowed release, I was allowed to move to the honor dorm where it was more relaxed. It was startling to discover that I maintained a clean record for that long. The attempted escape rendered no disciplinary infraction.

The truth of the matter was that I wasn't ready for release as I had been pursuing a successful career in playology and crimology. The desire

to obtain a successful job simultaneously
ensued, but my intentions in even that would
entail corruption.

At this stage in my life, it definitely wasn't
feasible for me to obtain employment as a bank
teller because of my corrupted behavior in
being the mastermind and inside man of the
bank being robbed. Nor was it feasible for me
to enter into law enforcement because of my
corrupted behavior of earning triple scale of
my actual earnings by taking some of the dope
of those I busted to give to the dope pushers
for my capitalization. Likewise, the medical
field was not an option because of the
corrupted behavior of marketing the accessible
drugs of the drug addict's choice.

On many occasions the contemplation of
escorting a corrupted behavior to a place of
employment rolled around my mind. But who
in their right mind would consider hiring me? I
was young, inexperienced, and uneducated.
Not to mention the fact of them discovering
that I had been incarcerated.

Although I was experiencing the battlefields of
incarceration, I pursued success by entering
into a trade school which taught auto
mechanics, printing, welding, woodworking

and upholstery trades. My aunt's unfortunate experiences with her cars motivated me to make auto mechanics my choice. It was a bad choice! The teacher was not interested in teaching. He was there to simply draw a check. Nevertheless, I made it a habit to ask questions, but the answers were unsatisfactory, so my stay there was short.

My next trade was welding. For those who showed an interest in learning, the welding teacher would teach, although there were times when I felt that he was too preoccupied to teach upon request. I primarily learned how to use a torch. And although I learned to weld on a metal plate, I never became good enough to weld anything together.

Someone had piqued my interest to take up printing where I learned more than I had in any other trade. The instructor and his assistant were extremely eager to teach. Much of what I remember is how I learned to transfer printed material from paper to a very thin sheet approximately 15 X 10 that would be attached to the wheel of a printing press. We were required to rub a substance on the sheet, put a tube of ink in the printer and a ream of paper, allowing it to run for a while in order for the ink to get on the sheet. Thereafter, printing commenced. I also learned how to develop film and make pamphlets.

Success in printing was promising, especially through the corrupted behavior of making counterfeit money, but I would never get the opportunity to use those skills under any circumstance. The voice of my tortured soul would hinder my progress to achieve anything accessible.

CHAPTER XI

TRAUMATIC VOICE.

Adequate time for verbal expression is extremely essential for those with traumatic experiences but often, the traumatic voice refuses to speak and trauma's victim travels life's journey as a deaf mute, yet along the way the sign language of the deaf mute is seen in behavior, but only understood by those who either know the signs from experience or by some form of education.

Fear of rejection, betrayal, embarrassment, pride, fear's slap in the face and distrust are contributing factors to the traumatic voice's refusal to speak and it is often difficult to persuade the traumatic voice to speak no matter what the experience or education. Love, kindness, patience, and proof of true concern are the proper tools for operation. And with her she possessed the proper tools. Although

she would need an extremely special tool to get
what I had locked away in the dungeon of my
soul.

Mary was a Caucasian woman who stood 5' 7".
She was about 23 or 24 years old, and was in
pursuit of education at one of the nearby
universities where she majored in psychology.

The boy's home administration was in need of
more counselors for some type of special
project. The four counselors selected for the
project were allowed to work part-time while
they continued their education.

At this particular juncture I was sixteen and
living in the honor dorm. I had been selected to
be part of Marys' caseload. Although she was
there as a counselor, she became more than just
a counselor to me. Many midmornings caught
us sitting under the shade of' a tree or in her
office sharing conversation. She would listen
intently to all I had to share.

I never knew, whether or not, her mother
abandoned her, but she would listen intently to
my traumatic voice as I expressed the hurt I
experienced due to my mother's abandonment
and rejection. She never discussed her father
turning his back on her, but she would listen
intently as I shared with her about my father

74

turning his back on me. She never talked about being incarcerated, but she would listen intently to my experience.

Her response primarily consisted of challenging me to rise above the circumstances lingering in my life. But how could I accomplish such when each day I would be greeted by past circumstances slapping me in the face?

I was on the verge of fast becoming a whore, pushed around by a circumstantial pimp and kicked in the middle of the street of life to be shaped into being what I had no desire to be.

Circumstances are not a defining principle of who we are, yet they are capable of shaping "what" we become. For instance: the circumstances of being neglected as a child can shape one into becoming a neglectful parent. One who experiences abuse can be shaped into becoming abusive. Being constantly told that you will never amount to anything can shape one into seeing no purpose for life. And too many of us have become what adverse circumstances escorted in our lives. Even me!

CHAPTER XII

NEW LIFE.

Over and over in my head played the many sad songs life forced me to dance to in the club of adversity. Living nightmares to influence the contemplation of seeking eternal sleep to awake from the torture, but how could I now contemplate such given the opportunity to hold the delicacy of new life in my arms as I would hold a bouquet of delicate, freshly picked flowers? Caressing my fingertips, encouraging a warm smile as a beholding gaze searched with bewilderment. Soothing lips from a gentle kiss, inspiring tears as a glorious sound of an escaping cry invades the air.

Innocence, someday robbed by life, where hope lived in me that the traumatic experiences I possessed would not creep upon him that would ensue admitting him in the hospital of life to be medicated by drugs and alcohol to escape the bitter torture of his soul.

Much too young I was for him, only seventeen, but he's my son, my precious son! There's more, I discovered, to being a father then simply having a child.

It was my desire to be a father, but how could I be a father when I didn't have a father to show me what fatherhood was all about? Where lies the appropriate time to show him how to walk? Or take him out as a father to play catch when father never took me out to play catch or showed me how to walk? When do I feed him or change him? What does it mean when he cries? Where lies the appropriate time to teach him about the little girls who would one day pique his interest? How to drive? How to fight? How to be a man, husband, father, provider, worker, save his earnings, make proper investments, seek education, how to be content with the pursuit of an honest way of living? Where lies the appropriate time to teach him about the survival in life under any circumstance?

The only thing I could teach him at this juncture was: how to be a failure, how to drop out of school, run from problems, steal, connive, scheme, smoke cigarettes and dope, drink and carry a gun. More than that, how to be incarcerated.

Matter of fact, I was incarcerated when he was conceived and during the period his mother carried him and on the day he was born. Even as I sat holding him in my arms, I was behind the bars of my decision. He needed me in freedom's light and I needed to be in freedom's light for him, for his mother, for us.

I had been told repeatedly, "Toby, don't get that girl pregnant!" But I wouldn't listen. I couldn't keep my hands off of her.

I had returned home on many occasions on leaves from the boy's home. My first leave was for a two week Christmas leave in 1981. I had been arrested on an unusual cold April's night in 1980. In order to prevent me from getting into any further criminal activity, I was allowed to spend each day of my leave with Janet, who I considered making my wife. I was allowed to go home every month for the weekend thereafter. Each time I was allowed to spend too much time with her, that is until it was discovered by her mother that she was pregnant. Then my leaves mysteriously ceased! I felt devastated. No more late night rendezvous because we didn't get enough of each other earlier during the day.

I had met Janet right before my armed robbery and attempted murder case. Her shyness was startling because I didn't know about sharing in conversation. The deafening sound of silence often visited us, but we survived and now we were parents with hopes to be married. Janet was fifteen when she became a mother.

But now, after Mary assisted me to acquire a spring leave, in 1982, that allowed me to be home for a week, I was about to make a run.

The possibility of scraping and scrounging a bit to eat lay ahead for us, but we'd survive. The probability of poor living conditions lay ahead, but we'd be together. Our appearance may appear sad, but we'd be happy with each other.

My steps were rapid as I made my way through the trail ways bus terminal like a paranoid schizophrenic. I was seeking seclusion.

The uniformed police officer gave me the impression that he was watching me in order to seize the right moment to apprehend me.

Although apprehension was an eventual possibility, such wasn't feasible when, in fact, I hadn't been missing long enough for my absence to be discovered. I believed that I had an approximate four to five hour head start.

I had left my family a note to make them aware of my intentions. Simply hoping they would be understanding. I knew my grandmother and grandfather wouldn't call the police, but my aunt, that was a different story.

I hurriedly walked up the stairs of the trail ways bus terminal to the bathroom, looking over my shoulder to see if anybody, aside from the police officer, was monitoring my movements to nab me at the allotted time.

On entering the bathroom, I stepped in one of the stalls, locking it behind me. I stayed behind the closed door, peering out through the cracks in the stall door to see who entered when hearing the opening of the bathroom door, as if I was playing the childhood game of hide and seek.

When I heard the announcement of the bus boarding to Houston. I hurriedly made my way through the ground level floor of the bus station. I watched closely for the policeman, who I discovered was nowhere in sight. Upon boarding the bus, I sat like a nervous child awaiting a whipping after being mischievous, hoping the bus driver would speed up the process of hole punching the tickets in order to get everyone boarded and the bus in motion.

Although my destination would be Houston, I knew no one there. My intention was to go to California because I believed that finding a job would be easy, especially for what I desired; to seek a musical career, but I didn't have enough money for the bus fare.

I had been able to acquire the money through a special work program in the boys home, cutting grass.

I was greeted by bright lights, big buildings, and beautiful scenery when the bus pulled into downtown Houston. Not exactly what I hoped for, not what I'd dreamed and definitely not what I anticipated.

The bright lights I had hoped for consisted of the lights of the entertainment industry.

The big buildings I dreamed of were the buildings that held thousands of screaming fans, their voices screaming, shouting, and speaking my name as I'd pour out to them songs from the depths of my heart. I had always believed that a big city was the place for me to effectively begin establishing a musical career, which was the primary reason I desired to go to California, but I quickly discovered that the streets of Houston possessed other plans.

Roaming and living on the streets of Houston was definitely not my primary intention. I thought a couple of days, perhaps three at the most would be sufficient before finding a place of employment and a place to live. I was confident in my street survival without either, but I now had a family. However, all I was able to acquire out of Houston was excessive street walking, looking over my shoulder for the apprehender and being hustled.

The hustle game of the street opened its doors as it had on many occasions during my street survival days, but I realized that the consequences of being caught were now a lot graver. I was older, and older meant years in prison that provided no special leaves like the one I had been given from the boy's home.

Problems are rampant in life, and we can create more in seeking the solution if we chose to handle it in a negative way. This is exactly what I had done in this situation.

Instead of being introduced to potential employers, the streets of Houston introduced me to a new hustle game, or at least new to me.

He had appeared to be lost and I had concluded that he was when I discovered that he spoke with a Jamaican accent. I immediately became captured and bound by the handcuffs of his hustle by displaying an interest in assisting him. He piqued my interest more when he revealed a sock and said that it was full of money, and he needed someone to hold his money in order to prevent the prostitute he would acquire from stealing it. Well, I figured that I was his man, surely, he can trust me.

It turned out that I had to reveal that I was trustworthy. He asked me how much money I had. I had about fifteen/twenty dollars. He told me that if I would trust him with my money, he felt that he could trust me with his. What I was to do was give him my money and walk around the block where we would meet, "That muthafucka got me!" I became hustler turned hustled. I realized after I made the block that —I had been had. I had explained that I was just passing through which gave him the impression that he would never see me again, but we wound up meeting again the next day. He claimed that he got caught up in

83

something that prevented him from meeting me. He promised that he would give me back my money. I was too tired to argue or put up any kind of a fight. I had been awake for two days. Matter of fact, as we were sitting on a downtown bench talking, I fell asleep. When I awoke he was gone. That was the last time I saw him.

Apparently I hadn't learned my lesson about running into someone who appeared to be lost. This particular man got off the bus looking around as though he had never seen the city before, so I asked him if he needed directions. He, instead, stuck his hand in his clothes as though he was going for a gun, and told me to turn around. As I slowly turned around I sought the direction I would run but there was no running place. Ahead of me was a construction site walkway that was straight. I couldn't run to the right or left. There was no hiding place. If I was going to get shot, I would have to stand my ground, but he told me to get out of his face.

Not only did I get out of his face, *I got out of the city.*

There was nothing there for me. I would have to hide in Dallas, a territory I was very familiar with. I had been afraid that the police would be looking for me in Dallas because my father's address was in their records.

CHAPTER XIII

HER HAUNTED HOUSE.

This particular return to Dallas provided me with relief. It was not my intention to return, but I had no choice. I had become bloated with the meal that the streets of Houston served.

After a night in the streets of Dallas, I discovered that the authorities were not looking for me through a telephone conversation I had with my stepmother. I felt even more relieved when I discovered through a telephone conversation with my aunt that the authorities in Louisiana had not inquired about me either.

I had also discovered through a telephone conversation with my aunt that my biological mother was living in Dallas. When I made contact with her, she provided me directions. She was living in West Dallas.

The entangling webs of the past permeated my mother's dwelling place where the furry legs of poison crept through the dark, dusty corners of her life, killing the hopes, dreams and desires of those connected to her. The structure of this building remains a mystery.

Conclusion could be drawn merely from speculation and the conclusion I considered is the dark deeds of trauma that burglarized the habitat of this termite infested dwelling place.

Fear of rejection, the fear of saying or doing the wrong thing in her presence accompanied those connected with her when merely considering coming in contact with her. In the dark night of her life, she had secretly opened the trap doors of abandonment to dump into the lives of others, those connected to her, as one would dump garbage into a dumpster.

On this particular occasion, a side of my mother was revealed to me that I hadn't recognized previously.

I had been disappointed that I was one of the eight she had given away, but now, I found myself grateful because I had the opportunity to see how I would have been treated, judging from the way she treated-my little brother and sister, the only two she had kept out of ten children. The question surfaced as to how a mother, who is supposed to be kind, loving and concerned for her children could dump eight of them unless she had been traumatized, or perhaps been adversely affected by some intoxicating substance, or was she insane? From observation, she treaded the shallow waters of them all.

 She had multiple personalities and appeared to be mad most of the time as she would often cruise the street of anti-socialism. Occasionally, the appearance of happiness would surface, which was normally triggered by the presence of other people or when she was dipping into the intoxicating drug of alcohol. The tone of her voice often revealed agitation when she was alone with her children. She would primarily hurl orders at us. "Do this!" "Do that!" There were no kind words, or words of encouragement. From this behavior it would appear that she hated our very existence.

I had hoped we could establish a mother-son relationship, but my primary concern at this point was for my new family and staying free of the apprehender. It was obvious, she had no interest in any relationship —at least not with her children.

She failed to provide food for her children even though she held a job at a restaurant. On many occasions she would leave her minor children alone at home while she was out partying or just simply hanging out at someone's house because of her disinterest in being at home. In her bedroom she had air conditioning and she would close her door, leaving her children in sweltering heat with a heat blowing fan in another room and would not allow them to turn it on when she was gone. When her air conditioner malfunctioned, she would allow her children to sleep in her room on the floor in order that she could have access to the fan. Occasionally, her daughter would gain the courage to request her to bring some food home. She would only bring enough for the evening for one person that three would have to share.

The refrigerator would normally contain ice, baking soda, dirt, and mildew... In the cabinets there would be sugar, flour, roaches and roach droppings. The house would stay in a mess. Clothes in the corners and middle of the floor. The toilet and bathtub were mildewed.

One night, after my street walking, when I came in, I discovered a pan of uncovered, cooked meat infested by roaches who dispersed upon my approach. I had left the house that night for more street walking, but when I returned, I discovered that all the meat disappeared. It was eaten by my little sister and her little friend. It was not feasible to see two little girls eating that amount of meat that was in that pan. I estimated it being enough for two muscle bound men who'd just worked on a construction site without having eaten anything during the day.

I was adversely affected by this. I had come seeking employment for the purpose of supporting my new family, but my priorities were disrupted.

Criminal behavior of stealing, robbing and burglary began to beckon me but the consequences, I realized, would lie in shallow wait and fail to tell the story of what lay beneath the surface to influence me to resort to such activities. Even the story, no matter how touching, would not allow the gavel of justice to extend any form of sympathy. Such criminal behavior would travel the halls of the judicial system where sympathy is not an option and mercy defies the law, especially for those who are financially unable to procure what the system deems as appropriate legal representation.

The birth of my son instilled in me the desire to make an honest living, but such was not available under the conditions I found myself in. There was no one I could turn to, so criminal behavior seemed my only option.

CHAPTER XIV

WAITING ARMS.

Carelessness, which came crashing down hard upon me, escorted the chains of justice into my life to take me captive once again, and escort me into the waiting arms of confinement.

Embarrassment hung my head in shame and burden weighed heavily on my heart. It wasn't supposed to turn out like this. I was now sitting behind the bars of Hurst, Texas city jail where the morning meal merely consisted of a donut and coffee and the afternoon meal consisted of a pot pie and juice. The evening meal consisted of a microwaved T.V. dinner and a camera to watch our every move.

The next day I was transferred to Tarrant County jail. My first day was a bit frightful. I was housed with other men and one of them troubled me by his constant stare.

"I hope I don't look like one of his girlfriends," I said to myself. My troubled thoughts were in turmoil. My nerves were on edge because I could visualize me receiving a lot more time behind bars if he contemplated me being his girlfriend. He was approximately six feet tall and two hundred pounds, therefore, a shank was definitely necessary.

This particular area housed approximately ten men. Two per cell. To the right of entering the tank were the cells. To the left was the dayroom where there were steel picnic tables and benches, a bathroom area that included shower, toilets and two sinks with mirrors above them. There was also a television in the dayroom.

I found the night, after our regulated bedtime, to be restless. I turned and twisted most of the night, wondering if I could take this man down in a matter of seconds like I'd seen in the movies, or would he take my attack with a smile and commence to beat me beyond recognition?

When I awoke the following morning for breakfast, I had fighting on my mind. I sat in a corner like a scared child on the verge of punishment with my fried eggs, oatmeal, biscuits, jelly and a half-pint milk. Everyone seemed to be at home as they enjoyed theirs and somebody else's breakfast.

The trusties would put the right amount of trays in the bean slots, which were approximately fifteen inches long and 5 inches wide. Whoever didn't come to get their tray of food was considered "stuck out."

"Williams," an officer called to me when they returned for the trays.

"Yea."

"Get all your things together, I'll be back to get you."

He definitely didn't need to tell me twice. The only thing I had to get was the extra pack of cigarettes and matches I had under my mattress. If it would have been a problem in me retrieving that, I would not have mind someone else smoking them.

When the officer returned, I was ready and raring to go. I really had no concern about where we were going as long as we were getting out of there.

As I was walking toward the door, I looked into the two-hundred pounders direction as he

94

was sitting in the dayroom. "Chump, you'll die a quick death fuckin' wit' me, "I mumbled loud enough for only me to hear.

Oh yes, I had instantly became Mister Big and Bad. I had some protection with the officer. And if Mr. "Two Hundred" would have made an unnecessary move, Mr. Officer would definitely earn his check peeling this big slab of flesh off me for taking a charge to him. But on the other hand, Mr. Officer would have probably run, leaving me to get a massive beating.

I was escorted to another area of the jail. I had discovered by the officer that I was supposed to be in a single cell. The officer that had me placed in the tank with other men had made a mistake. Although I was now eighteen, I was still considered a juvenile because I was under a juvenile sentence. Juveniles aren't allowed to be with adult prisoners.

Mary, who maintained contact with me while I was on the run, warned me to be careful with my job search. I was able to maintain contact with her via telephone and she had advised me how and who I should approach about a job which was basically no one.

"Be careful about accepting a job that pays with checks," I remember her saying. "Checks are easily traced."

The employment I was finally able to acquire led to my apprehension.

The music from Dallas' most popular black radio station, K-104, had played softly in the background as I walked through an area of the mall, mentally shopping for clothes. Then came an announcement that piqued my interest. Although it was a strain to hear, I was able to catch enough to learn that there was a job offer for salesmen. The announcement sent my feet racing to my father's house where I had returned after my short stay with my mother, in order to gather all the information concerning the advertisement I had heard. I

I had discovered that there was no experience required and that the agency would provide all training necessary. I especially liked the part where we would travel all over the United States.

I met with members of the agency that following day in a hotel, who asked me if I would be able to travel as well as start the following day. Upon affirmation, they provided me with an address where I could meet them the next morning.

Approximately eight to ten of us boarded a van in route to Arlington, Texas, where we were required to stay in a hotel, dormitory style. In the room where I was required to stay, there were two beds. One of the queen size beds was used by a guy who was with the agency for a while. Another young man and I who arrived together, were told to use the other available bed. I was skeptical about sleeping in the same bed with this guy. I guess the young man saw my reluctance.

"Hey man," he began. "You can choose either side, I don't care. I just want to get some sleep. We got to rise early in the morning. Don't worry man, I sleep on my side of the bed."

The following morning about one-hundred-fifty employees were required to meet in a large room. The heads of the agency explained our procedure for the day, the fact that we only get paid by commission. I was given an insurance type book full of order slips for the customers to order different type of magazines and encyclopedias.

My job consisted of excessive walking, knocking on doors and trying to convince people to purchase what I was selling. I was sent out with another guy who was supposed to be a veteran in this so-called game of salesmanship. "Just watch," I remember him saying as we approached the first door. I found it hilarious watching him attempt to convince someone to make an order for something they weren't interested in buying.

We were required to work for 12 hours a day and at days end if we didn't have any money or failed to make any sales, we would receive ten dollars. I would usually purchase something to eat, a pack of cigarettes and a quart of beer to help me to get to sleep, due to my restlessness.

There was a van to take us out to the area where we would solicit customers. The driver would designate a time and place to meet him at days end. Despite the weather conditions, which were normally cold, I considered this particular day delightful because I had the opportunity to work with an attractive young lady. It was a Friday and I had planned to find a party, some smooth liquor, marijuana and possibly a hot woman after work, preferably her. We would be off on Saturday and headed to another city on Sunday. Our next stop would be Utah, a place I had never visited, therefore, I considered celebrating appropriately.

The young lady and I decided to split up when we realized that we weren't accomplishing anything as a team, but splitting up was a mistake for me. Not only was I unsuccessful in making any sales, I had to face law enforcement's inquiry concerning my purpose for being in an apartment complex selling merchandise .

The first day of work I realized the danger of facing the apprehender. Every neighborhood we would go to someone would call the police who would question us about having a soliciting permit. Although the young lady and I had a soliciting permit, I failed to take it into my possession which resulted in my apprehension.

"Excuse me," the policeman said as he got out of his vehicle.

"Yea, what is it?" I questioned in an attempt to appear bold.

"I got a call that there were some solicitors in the area."

"Who?"

"Are you selling anything?"

"Yea."

"Well, I need to see your permit."

"I'm out with a young lady, she has the permit."

"Where is she?"

"There she is over there, she's over there," I said as I pointed to the young lady standing in one of the tenants' doorway in her attempt to make a sale.

We awaited the young lady's arrival, but she disappeared, leaving me stranded. I felt like someone had walked out of my life to drop me in the pig pen of life.

When the officer noticed that she disappeared, he requested my identification.

"Here you are," I said as I handed him my identification. I gave it to him without hesitation in the hope that it would persuade him to believe that I had nothing to hide, but it didn't work.

"He's not going to call," I tried to convince myself as he started walking toward his vehicle. "He's just trying to see if I'm bluffing."

"Put your hands on the car," the policeman said as he stormed out of his car with his hand on his weapon. "You're a wanted man."

He searched me, handcuffed me and walked me to the back seat of his police vehicle, a situation I was all too familiar with.

Although my identification card was fake, I was smart enough to have my real name on name on it. I only changed my age to get into clubs and for purchasing liquor. I never expected to be in this position regarding an ID.

This incident, of course, resulted in my return to the boys home although I would not return to the same one.

CHAPTER XV

RIDIN' HIGH

Aboard my first plane, I sat next to the window with the excitement of a child. Although I was excited, disappointment accompanied me because I realized that an extended portion of imprisonment lay ahead. Although I quickly grew tired of incarceration, I experienced problems in staying out of its way. We had grown close and I was well on my way to getting better acquainted.

My excitement quickly subsided upon discovering the awaiting chains of justice. The Baton Rouge law enforcement awaited the complete stop of the plane in order to bound me with their chains. My thoughts returned to the moment I was about to board the plane in Fort Worth. When the man who drove me to the airport had already left before I boarded the plane, I considered running, but was wary of the traps that could entail fatal consequences. Perhaps another opportunity to run existed, I thought.

But now that I was walking toward the awaiting chains, I wished I had made a run for it, as I noticed the proud looks on their faces. There were two uniformed officials and one officer dressed in plain clothes. As they began to handcuff and shackle me, I began to imagine the look on their faces if I, their prisoner, had not gotten off the plane. Looking in all directions in bewilderment, they'd find themselves racing to the nearest phone. But I failed to provide them with the opportunity and my failure contributed to my return to the trenches of incarceration.

The stay in the Diagnostic center, where I was taken for a battery of physical and psychological tests, seemed like three months, although it was only three weeks. On this occasion I experienced more outside activity.

I was now 18, and due to my age, I was not allowed to return to Monroe. I was sent to Scotlandville, which is located in the same area of diagnostic.

I could only hope that things would be better, although this facility was considered to be more dangerous. There were more fights, stabbings and killings.

Expecting to step through the front door of my first confrontation, I surprisingly found the dorm I was assigned to be relaxed. I attributed it to the fact that since the young men were older, they were a bit more mature. All of us were eighteen and older.

In the sleeping area the beds were lined up down two sides of the area approximately 3 feet apart. To the left facing the bedroom area was a wall, and to the right were windows. The beds on each side were approximately 5 feet apart which left space for walking through. On the opposite end of the bedroom area was a bathroom. Since I had just arrived, I had the misfortune of sleeping close to the entrance where the light shone in my face and where the officers post was located.

I lived in dorm for about six months. I was eventually moved to the honor dorm, which was more relaxed.

Disappointment would often visit and come knocking on my door.

CHAPTER XVI

CRUSHING

Often crushing experiences escort us back to reality after we've lost our focus and in losing our focus we find ourselves straying into the field of abandonment. Abandoning our responsibilities to leave with someone else to take care of.

Crushings have sent many dope fiends in the tumbling effect of "cold turkey," have broken the bottle of many drunks, ripped the immoral mattress of homosexuality, and have run the prostitute from the whoring corner of the street. Crushings have sent unfaithful spouses to kneel in tears apologetically, have caused the neglectful father or mother to return to their responsibilities of raising their children. Crushings have a tendency to snap back into reality those who have lost focus and I believed that crushing delivered reality to my father. He had suffered a series of six or seven strokes. I witnessed his pitiful condition whilst I was on the run from the boy's home. He had been bedridden for some time, I was told, but when I went to live with him I discovered that he was up walking with the aid of an aluminum cane. His whole right side had been paralyzed. Although things weren't as they should have been in our relationship, I never hated him. I had believed that we would eventually establish a father-son relationship.

I had obtained a driver's education permit when I was in Monroe boy's home and I used to drive my father's camper. He always loved to fish and there were times, it seemed, he would go out of state to where he heard the fish were biting. Although silence remained deafening between us, I enjoyed having the opportunity to take him fishing. He would often have four to five rods and reels cast in the water and about two fishing poles, while he sat on the bank with a fishing pole in his hand. Whatever he'd catch he would take home and my stepmother would seem to take joy in cooking it. This was the fondest memory I had of my father and to see the gleam in his eyes and the smile of contentment when he noticed a fish caught in the traps of his rod and reels or on one of his fishing poles.

As I sat in the boy's home reminiscing, it occurred to me that my father and I would never get the opportunity to fish together again. The discovery was made through a letter I received from Tina, the young girl I met on the run. Daddy was gone! With him he took away the opportunity we might have had to grow closer. He took the opportunity we might have had to ride around town, to share in sporadic conversations, to establish a meaningful father and son relationship. With him he took a part of me that was bound by joy just to be in his presence, a part of me that longed to jump into his arms, so he could caress and hold his little boy, to calm his fears and wipe away his tears, the little boy who terrorized for attention.

The tears from my father's death streamed down my face leaving stains of what could have been; what should have been. Daddy had left time for eternity, leaving a "grown boy" to continue in his quest for a father figure or just someone to care enough to manifest this "grown boy's" purpose in life.

CHAPTER XVII

HYPNOTIC POISON

In the gutter many have lain, driven by the pressures of life, to seek comfort or just a simple escape, only to be drawn into a hypnotic state the incapacitates and leaves it victim wallowing in the horrific septic system of life to drift into the path of destruction. Its odor stuns yet draws into its clutches the vulnerable, the tired, the weak, those who are basically fed up with life. There are those who are simply desiring to appear to be something different to what they have become and those who simply desire a social outlet. I fit in every category.

The astounding percentage of those addicted to this poison primarily revealed the slums' infestation of such behavior but there are a large percentage of isolated participants that abide in the upper echelon of life; strung out on the outer darkness of chemical's dependence. There are those who lie in wait seeking compensation for this hypnotic poison and I had become one of them. I knew the effects of what I was selling, therefore, my sales pitch could lure those without experience into its hypnotic grips by providing a captivating mental picture of its capabilities but for those who I knew would be my customers, I was required to merely persuade them to accumulate the funds I needed to get started.

There were young men on the compound residing in a drug rehabilitation dorm. I had become acquainted with three of them and when I made them aware of my intentions, they had no hesitation in bringing my plan to fruition.

In the dorm where I resided were a couple of young men who attended Southern University. They were allowed to leave each week day morning to pursue further education and would return each evening without being severely searched. Just what I needed. After accumulating the $10.00 I needed, I gave it to one of them to purchase marijuana. I had no interest in making a lot of money. My primary concern was to make back the $10.00 for the purpose of purchasing more of the marijuana to smoke. The only payment my connection desired was for me to give a couple to him and smoke with him. For $10.00 he would bring me a small sandwich bag that allowed me to roll about 15-20 marijuana cigarettes out of it at $2.00 apiece. I would only smoke with my connection, those I was close to or those I knew would return the favor.

Although there was no cocaine, no amphetamines, or heroin, I was setting myself up for selling even those products through the experience I was getting through the on-the-job training I was receiving in selling the marijuana. In the event legal employment had no interest for me, after my release, the illegal, black market would always reveal its "Help Wanted" sign.

Popularity and prestige embraced me as I cruised the corridors of the boy's home with the hypnotic poison. I had not anticipated such, but I was enjoying it. For the first time in my life I had begun to feel important. Many had begun to look up to me and respect me. I could hold my head up. Although it was all a facade, it made no difference. I was always required to dance to someone else's tune but now people were dancing to mine.

Sometimes guys would make an illegal move through their visit for marijuana and they would look me up to smoke with me and give me some for the purpose of selling. My job allowed me to cruise the school's corridors unhampered, without a written pass. Practically all the teachers knew I worked for the music teacher, Ms. Williamson, and their admiration for her allowed me to even hang out in their classrooms.

The majority of mornings would find me in a secluded area in order to take the hypnotic poison into my system. I considered this a great start to the day but things were slow at this particular time. Security tightened up on those leaving the campus for school. Every once in a while someone would possess the intestinal fortitude to smuggle some of the poison in after their weekend leave and that someone turned out to be my new locker partner who was from Baton Rouge. He asked me to meet him upstairs in the bathroom for a smoke of marijuana. I did not hesitate. Right in the middle of our smoke, the bathroom door opened. Busted! The officer said nothing. He simply looked at us and left. Since he said nothing, I believed that he would do nothing but we had a surprise awaiting us on our return downstairs.

"Y'all can go with him," he told us.

"Well, at least we can go to lock up high," I said jokingly as the disciplinary unit officer escorted us to the building right behind the honor dorm.

The disciplinary unit was on one floor. We were required to sit on the floor in silence from about six in the morning until about eight at night. We would shower and thereafter go to bed. This was our daily routine. Our meals were brought to us.

We were only required to stay in the disciplinary unit for 3 days and allowed to return to the honor dorm afterward.

I lived in the Baton Rouge boys' home a year and seven months. I had eventually started announcing my departure. "I'm going home tomorrow," I would often say. It appeared as though my words gave power to my constant announcement.

One day I was allowed to call my aunt who informed me that she would be coming to pick me up the next day —I was going home.

CHAPTER XVIII

TIRED LOSER.

Her words were annoying as they escaped her lips to impress on me the advice I had no interest in hearing. Something bout staying out of trouble. That old "stay out of trouble" speech from my aunt was worn and tired. I had hoped she would disregard giving that "stay out of trouble" speech, because it seemed the more she said it, the more I got into trouble.

I had discovered that a parole officer pressed the judge to release me on parole, According to my aunt, although the judge didn't believe I was ready, he only allowed it based on the parole officers persistence.

"I'll show him," I said to myself. "I'm more than ready!"

I had no concrete plans as to what type of job I would pursue. It really didn't matter as long as I was working and taking care of my responsibilities. I had already failed my son and his mother when I was on the run, but I had determined that I would not travel that road again. I wanted better for them, for all of my family. Besides, I was tired and wanted better for myself. I was now nineteen years old, tired of running from the law, riding in the backseat of police vehicles, uncomfortably handcuffed, tired of having nothing, of getting nowhere in life, jeopardizing my life, having my freedom snatched away, tired of boys pursuing me sexually, of waking up behind the fences of incarceration, tired of eating only what I had no interest in, tired of sleeping in the room with other young boys, going to bed when someone told me, working for free, tired of having to shower with other people, of having to use the bathroom with a room full of people, being told when and where to go, having to do other than what I desired.

I had been swinging on incarceration's door since I was twelve, running into the same old sad, troubled faces. I was determined to make a new start. I had entered a state of lunacy — doing the same old things and expecting different results. My behavior was doing nothing but cause me to lose. Lose out on experiencing life, growing into manhood, lose

114

out on being active in my son's life, on being a
husband to his mother who had gone her way.
I had lost her. She had got married and I
couldn't blame her for desiring to achieve
something out of life. I had held her up and
contributed to destroying her life. She was only
fifteen when she became pregnant, thus
causing her to have to drop out of school.

Although she moved on with her life, she
would come with my aunt, grandmother, and
grandfather to visit me after my apprehension
and with her she would bring our son. It was
always a delight to see them, but to see them
would deliver sadness to my heart because
inside I knew that we were supposed to be
enjoying life together in freedom's light, but I
had let them down --I failed them.

How can any male claim manhood when they
fail to stand as a man? I had no right to even
entertain the thought of claiming such when I
had so horribly failed to stand as a man. A real
husband is a man! A real father is a man! Any
male can say they are a husband and/or father,
but anyone simply saying they are a husband
and/or father carry no weight. It takes
backbone! Backbone in action.

Too many of us for far too long have walked out on our responsibilities, primarily because we're functioning with a slave mentality. During those physical slavery days that our forefathers endured, they were ordered to animalistically mate with their women in order that the slave owner could take the child and have him raised up in slavery. They were merely required to make the child, not worry about taking care of it. We're continuing to function in that mentality, giving our children over to being raised in modern day slavery to drugs, alcohol and the material things of life. This has contributed to the nation's fears. Fear of the many angry young men who dangerously lurk the streets for victims who are controlled by their slave masters.

At this particular juncture, I would have another opportunity to be a father. I would have the opportunity to step out of my slave mentality and function as a human being. Although I had lost the chance of being my son's mother's husband, I maintained the desire to stand by her. She had given up so much for me and our son and received so little.

The area was full of businesses which were close to my aunt's home. I went to approximately 9-10 out of about fifteen, in

search of employment, but it was apparent that
parolee was written all over me because I was
unsuccessful in procuring employment. I filled
out applications and spoke with some of the
employers, but nothing looked promising and I
was given the impression by them that they
were not interested because they would
interrupt me in the middle of what I was
saying to them. Although I was a high school
dropout and on parole, I would merely tell
them that I had graduated and had been to a
trade school in Monroe, where I took classes in
auto mechanics, welding, printing and
upholstery. The only thing I ended up with out
of this search was unemployment's depression.

All the "ifs" I had accumulated over the years
started to roll around in my thoughts. If
education had been important enough for me
to graduate, procuring employment wouldn't
have been as difficult. If I hadn't had a death
defying love for money, I wouldn't be a
parolee. If I hadn't been careless, I wouldn't
have had a son out of wedlock to be
responsible for. If I hadn't been concerned
about running with those hoodlum friends of
mine I would have learned a lot more during
school. Ifs can accomplish nothing, therefore,
when the opportunity presents itself to

accomplishing something to be successful, it would be extremely wise to take advantage of it.

Lack of education sent my mother into a restaurant to wait tables, it sent my aunt into different homes and office buildings as a maid, it sent my grandmother into different homes to take care of the helpless elderly, my father into digging ditches in the field of construction and my grandfather into different types of low class jobs. Now, lack of education was on the verge of sending me back into the streets to bob and steal.

The only jobs, it seemed, available for me was in the arms of incarceration. There I had no problem in procuring employment. As a matter of fact, a job is available without having to search for it. Although it may not be the desired job, one is available and there are no applications to be concerned with. There are seldom any interviews that ask about former experiences or education. In the vast majority of places of confinement, the job pays either good time or nothing at all. Those that do, pay no more than five dollars a day, but most of that goes on expenses.

But now, as I stood on the bank of
discouragement with a cloud of smoke
lingering above my head fcom my cigarette, I
considered reverting back to what I knew.
Hustle!

CHAPTER XIX

HUSTLE !

It was a usual party night for me with Kenneth and Master Tom. Kenneth had got too drunk to keep up, therefore, Master Tom and I ditched him. We left him in an old abandoned car in an area in Shreveport call Motown with the intentions of returning to pick him up the next morning.

I had met Kenneth prior to going to the boys home in Monroe. Kenneth was a stocky built man who stood about 6'2", about 202 pounds. He was considered to be an ox strong country boy. He worked in construction digging ditches. He loved to get drunk, and in his drunken state of being he would love to either fight, eat, or sleep.

I met Master Tom after my release on parole. Master Tom was a mild-mannered man, that is until he got drunk. His drunken state of being would lead him to becoming verbally abusive. His drinking and psychiatric medication wouldn't mix well. What I noticed was that he was capable of following instructions in criminality. I only picked up on this through his conversations as to how other would tell him to do something, and he would do it without question. This particular night, I would get the opportunity to witness it.

Master Tom and I had some hustling to do and Kenneth's drunken state would disrupt us. There was money to be made.

The victims we found were hunting for something in the grass behind a club while their car set running idle nearby with the doors open. I gave Master Tom an order to make them aware that we would be relieving them of their car. As he pointed the gun in the man and woman's direction, they simply watched in amazement without a word.

Master Tom definitely meant business, I observed, as he approached the car in a semi squatting position like a cop easing upon an armed criminal, prepared to fire a shot.

Master Tom began driving off wildly before I had the chance to close the door of the continental. As he made a sharp turn in the parking lot, he began hollowing like a cowboy, "Yeeeee haw." Just as he'd made the cowboy expression, the gun went off in his hand while he was trying to hold it along with using the same hand to turn the steering wheel.

"Man! what the fuck you doing? You trying to kill us?" I stated, not really concerned about him shooting himself.

Although I knew he was familiar with the area, I gave him directions to the interstate since the liquor obviously affected his thinking.

His intentions were to joyride. I would have been okay with that, but not with this car. A stolen car would reap minor charges if apprehended but the charges in this car had risen to a level of armed robbery, therefore, we would be considered armed and dangerous and there was bound to be an all points bulleting out on the car.

Master Tom could easily get off the hook for being insane since he was under psychiatric care. But I was on parole, and surely be considered the master mind of this crime.

After we parked the car in the woods, where Master Tom and I rummaged it. There were a quite a few clothes and small appliances. We carried what we could to David's house nearby. There were enough clothes in the back seat and trunk to start a small garage sale. The appliances consisted of an electric heater, small vacuum, iron that didn't require an ironing board and a .357 magnum.

The expression on David's face revealed irritation at being awakened at this hour, but he soon got over his anger when he noticed the items we possessed were worth money.

David and Kenneth were brothers. I met and hung out with David before my juvenile life sentence. We all lived in the same neighborhood.

We spent a few hours going through the clothes, drinking, smoking marijuana, playing video games, all for the purpose of wasting a little time to await daybreak in order to pick up David's brother, Kenneth.

Upon our arrival in Motown, we met Kenneth walking. Although it was a very long walk ahead for Kenneth, it wasn't new to him as he had done this on many occasions.

"Yea, I know man, we shouldn't have left you," I began when noticing his hesitation on getting into the car as I held the door open for him.

"Y'all tripped out on me man."

He eventually got in the-car. As soon as he took his sip of alcohol, his anger quickly subsided.

Most of the items we sold from the car went up in smoke and into the drainage pipes.

CHAPTER XX

FREAKY BEHAVIOR

Approximately two to two and a half months had passed, and I had been doing pretty well with the curfew that my aunt established for me, to be in before midnight, but I started going over my time gradually. Ten minutes late, twenty minutes. When I was up to about an hour she expressed concerns about it. I don't remember exactly what she said, something about coming in later and later. I would often ignore her because she could take hours to explain something which was always annoying to me.

The time I was required to be in was when the party would go into full swing. It was the time that the freaky behavior of those loving the influence of the night would come out. The night influenced those in hiding to be who they really desired to be, to do the things they really desired to do without being concerned about daylight catching them in the act.

My sexual desire was spreading like fire, blazing out of control and the only way I believed I could extinguish it was by finding someone who was influenced by the night with a freaky behavior. Such behavior required no extensive wining and dining to acquire a sexual escapade. It required no long conversations, no long walks or establishing a relationship. Freaky behavior has lured many into unplanned parenthood, it had led many into acquiring deadly diseases. I had already entered into the lustful state of unplanned parenthood and now I was on my way to contracting a venereal disease.

It was obvious, she was one influenced by the night. Her attire consisted of a halter top that barely covered her large breasts and shorts so short that revealed the bottom part of her buttocks.

"Say, look out Ken., who that?" I questioned when I approached him standing in the yard of his construction employer.

"That's Denise, you don't won't none ah dat."

"I don't know why in the fuck not!"

He walked closer to me and told me that he'd heard that the young woman had a disease.

Well, I was going to have to find out for myself given the opportunity. I'm sure it wasn't nothing ole doc couldn't take care of if I caught something from her.

"She stuck up too," Kenneth stated.

I had discovered that Denise was living next door to David, Kenneth's brother, who was now living with Kati, a Caucasian woman who used to live next door to my aunt. I had the opportunity to meet her during my Christmas leave from the Baton Rouge boy's home in 1983.

Hanging around David and Kati's house would give me the opportunity to pursue Denise who was living with Vera in Vera's father's house next door. I used to speak to Vera occasionally when I was younger but I hadn't seen her since 1982, during my spring leave from Monroe's boy's home.

I would walk around her as though she didn't exist, wearing my cheapest best clothes and expensive, stolen cologne.

"Yea, get a whiff of that!" I would say to myself.

My efforts begun to look promising when one day she approached me while I was on David and Kati's porch crushing ice.

"Hey," she began when she approached me. "I've been seeing you around here a lot, you live around here?"

"Yea, I said, trying to conceal my excitement. "I live a couple of streets over."

"Well, I just thought I would speak to you," she concluded.

After I expressed a desire to see her again, she left. I went into David and Kati's house feeling like I had just won a trophy. This was the beginning of our relationship.

I later discovered through sharing conversation with her on another occasion that she was romantically involved with one of Vera's brothers who was in prison. Well, I had determined, I would keep her warm until he got out, that's of course if I could prevent her from putting her hooks-in-me. I was unsuccessful.

"Let's go inside," Denise told me one night when I was sitting on the trunk of a car in Vera's yard drinking and smoking marijuana with Kenneth, Vera, and Vera's fiancé.

I couldn't get off the car quickly enough to accompany her. I thought of what Kenneth told me about the possibility of her having a disease, but first things first. I waited far too long for this moment to jeopardize it by questioning her about anything concerning a disease. The desire to quench my lustful desires outweighed my concern for my health and such desires have called many to an early grave. Although AIDS was in existence, I didn't believe that the epidemic reached our neighborhood. Whether it had or not, for the moment, it was time to get my freak-on.

CHAPTER XXI

MYSTERIOUS WOMAN

One of Vera's brothers lived next door to my aunt's house with his wife who was celebrating his birthday with drinking, smoking marijuana, refreshments and dancing. Denise and I were invited by Vera to accompany her and her fiancé. Denise and I had grown sexually close but division, it seemed, would be on the verge of driving us apart when this mysterious woman sat next to me. She appeared to be distant, but she was very attractive and if Denise wasn't around I would introduce myself. It was a struggle to say nothing to her.

The voice that escaped her lips were soft. "Would you like to dance?" The mysterious woman questioned.

Denise would just have to be upset, but she said nothing. Neither did she possess the inkling of anger, she simply watched.

The mysterious woman danced gracefully as her silver tooth smile glittered under the dim light. After our dance she disappeared, leaving me in question as to "What was her name?" "Where did she come from?" "Where did she live?" "Is she married?" "Does she have any relatives around?" "Was she one influenced by the night?"

My body spent most of the night with Denise, but my mind was on the mysterious woman.

The domino game was in progress when Kenneth and I joined the party, at Betty's house a few nights after meeting the mysterious woman. I had only met Betty after my parole. She had brought some party flavor to the neighborhood when she moved in with her brother. There were dominoes, liquor, marijuana and blues music almost every night. On this particular night the mysterious woman was sitting at the domino table with Betty as her partner. After about half an hour of building up my courage, I eased up behind her and asked, "Do you remember me?"

"Yes, you're my dancing partner," she responded.

I discovered that her name was Joyce who lived about three houses down from Betty, which was a surprise. I went to school with her sisters Patricia and Lisa and my aunt knew her mother for about thirty years.

"How old do you think I am?" She questioned suddenly after she asked me to walk her home.

"About 26, 27?" I guessed.

"I'm 32."

I was speechless. "Okay, okay, I'll play it cool. She got to have something up her sleeve," I said to myself.

"Hey, look, it wouldn't work between us. You're young and I would have a hard time keeping up with you."

My goodness, the girl don't waste no time, definitely one of the night.

"I could maybe by your god-mother or something."

She suddenly struck a nerve, "Look, I don't need a mama. The one I have don't do me no damn good." She only smiled and changed the subject.

"All men want out of women is sex," she blurted.

I'll show her that I'm not merely after sex, although I was.

Joyce enjoyed taking early morning walks. Although my presence wasn't required, I offered to accompany her. I learned that she had just moved from Dallas, after a divorce, with her mother and father.

My aunt, grandmother and grandfather loved her and enjoyed her company. Although my aunt had determined that she wouldn't allow me to have any more young ladies in the house after Janet's pregnancy, she made an exception with Joyce.

Although I continued in a relationship with Denise, me and Joyce's relationship blossomed and bloomed to the degree that we discussed marriage. And often times my aunt would refer to her as my wife. But the result of my criminal activity would intervene and contribute to preventing me from doing such. I would find myself cornered, to travel the halls of justice instead of travel the aisle of holy matrimony.

THE CRIME.

***Due to impending investigations, and the statue of limitations, the Author does not wish to go into detail with a personal account of the events that led up to the next chapter. The following is an excerpt from the official transcript from the inmate's trial v. the State of Texas.

Out of respect for the deceased and their families, the names of the names of the victims have been edited out of the transcript, along with the real names of the female criminals, who have been referred to thus far in the book as "Denise" and "Vera".

773 S.W.2d 525 (1988)

Toby Lynn WILLIAMS, Appellant, v. The STATE of Texas, Appellee Court of Criminal Appeals of Texas, En Banc. June 22, 1988...

Toby Lynn Williams was convicted of murdering (VICTIM) while in the course of kidnapping or attempting to kidnap her. The testimony of the witnesses at the guilt/innocence stage of the trial revealed the following facts concerning this offense. At around 9:30 or 10:00 p.m. on the night of December 19, 1984, (CODENAME DENISE) and (CODENAME VERA) left (VERA'S) home to go for a walk in their hometown of Greenwood, Louisiana, a town about 15 miles from the Texas border. The purpose of their walk was to get some cigarettes, but during their walk they encountered Toby Lynn Williams (THE AUTHOR), As the two women approached a bridge near (VERA'S) house they came upon the defendant squatting down near the street, holding a .357 magnum pistol. The defendant asked the two women, with whom he was acquainted, whether "they wanted to make a couple of thousand dollars" by robbing a

[773 S.W.2d 527]

man at his house on Rice Road, which was nearby.

The three of them agreed to carry out the robbery, but first they decided to go to the house of a friend of (VERA'S) to get some cigarettes. While at this friend's house they smoked marihuana, and talked, and finally went to the store for some beer and cigarettes in the car of another friend who had driven by, (NAME PROTECTED) They made their purchases, and after sitting in the car smoking marihuana and listening to music,

(VERA, DENISE, and TOBY) left the car walking with (FRIEND). (FRIEND) soon left the three of them and walked back to his own house. The planned robbery was not discussed by the three of them in the presence of their other friends.

After (FRIEND) left them, (DENISE, VERA, AND TOBY) walked to the house on Rice Road. It was approximately 11:30 p.m. when defendant knocked on the door while holding the pistol under his jacket. (MALE VICTIM) came around from a side entrance after turning on the outside lights. (MALE VICTIM) asked how he could help the defendant. Defendant then pulled his gun and told (MALE VICTIM) to get inside the house and turn off the outside lights. Defendant made (MALE VICTIM) go back into his bedroom, where his wife, (FEMALE VICTIM), and their six month old child were. Defendant demanded to know where (MALE VICTIM'S) money and jewelry were located, but (MALE VICTIM) only had about eleven dollars in cash with him. Defendant then asked if he had any guns and proceeded to collect his shotgun, 30-30, and 22 rifle, which the two women thereafter kept trained on the (VICTIMS).

Defendant then asked him if he had money in the bank, and demanded his automatic teller machine card to get access to the funds. He told him how to use it to withdraw the one hundred and ten dollars which was in his savings account. Defendant took the keys to his car and left to remove the funds from the account at an

137

automatic teller machine, leaving (DENISE AND VERA) to guard the (VICTIMS) While the defendant was gone, (DENISE AND VERA) alternately collected items of personal property from around the house and put them in pillow cases, while the other stood guard. The defendant was unable to get any money from (VICTIM'S) account by using the automatic teller card. He and the two women proceeded to load goods from the house into the truck, including a stereo and a console television, which Toby made the victim help him load. During this time the victim determined that the defendant was Toby Lynn Williams, a former employee of his.

Upon his return from attempting to get the money from the victim's account, Williams told (DENISE) that they would have to kill (MALE AND FEMALE VICTIM) because they would be witnesses in a police investigation. After (TOBY, DENISE AND VERA) loaded up the truck with goods, the defendant told the victims to get dressed because they had to go with him to "take care of some business." It was then around 2:30 a.m. on the morning of December 20, 1984. With (DENISE AND VERA) in the front seat, and (VERA) holding the .357 magnum pistol on the victims, who were in the back seat, Williams drove out to a relatively deserted road just across the border inside the Texas state line, some 15 miles from the victim's house. The defendant then told the victims to get out of the car and give their six-month-old son to (DENISE). When (FEMALE VICTIM) refused to give up her child, (DENISE) slapped her to try to make her obey. (FEMALE

VICTIM) finally relinquished the child to her husband, who handed the baby over to (DENISE)

(VERA AND DENISE) returned to the car with the baby while Williams made the victims walk down the road from the car.

The defendant then told them to take off their clothes and "make love" to each other standing up.

When the couple was unable to do so, the defendant ordered them to *lie down on the street and have intercourse.*

Again, the victims were not able to comply. While they knelt in the street facing each other, hugging and crying, wearing only their undergarments, Williams raised the 30-30 and shot (FEMALE VICTIM) through the middle of her back.

The bullet exited her body immediately below her bra, and entered her husband's body.

[773 S.W.2d 528]

The victims then fell to the ground immediately adjacent to one another.

The defendant proceeded to move (MALE VICTIM) into a ditch on the side of the road which was filled with weeds. He then tried to do the same with (FEMALE VICTIM), but was unable to do so, apparently because her weight was too great. Upon returning to the car, The defendant said that they would have to shoot (MALE VICTIM) again because he was not going to die from the wound which he had sustained. (DENISE) suggested that he would indeed die from the wound without shooting him again. The defendant then got in the car, pulled up to where the bodies were and shined the car headlights on each of them.

The three then drove off with the baby in the car.

The defendant pulled over at a house on the side of the road and left the baby on the porch of the house.

(TOBY, DENISE AND VERA) then returned to the neighborhood in which they and the victims lived. They abandoned the car in some woods located near Hinton's house, and ran through the woods. Although they had planned to go back to the victims' house to get the truck which they had loaded with goods, they decided not to do so when they heard sirens close by. Instead, (TOBY, DENISE AND VERA) ran back to (VERA'S) trailer home where they hid until the police came to investigate. Meanwhile, at the scene, (MALE VICTIM) managed to get up out of the ditch and walk to a house to obtain help. The victim was able to tell the police the name of his assailant. While (MALE VICTIM) was gone to get help, his wife, (FEMALE VICTIM) died as a result of the gunshot wound inflicted on her by the defendant.

CHAPTER XXII

CORNERED.

The sound of crushing leaves echoed in the night with each step Vera, Denise, and I made as we ran through the woods from the apprehending hand of the law.

We made it back to Vera's trailer to hide with fear as our companion. Vera joined her boyfriend and her little girls in the living room. I found myself a place on the floor of one of the small rooms to retrieve a cigarette, When Denise joined me, I took her in my arms without a word.

Vera had moved in the trailer a short time after my release, which stood on the same property of her father. It had now become our fortress.

I had begun to count myself out; down for the court, and soon the game of life would be over for me in freedom's light. I couldn't go back to incarceration, I considered, but there was no more running, no way out — I was cornered! I could feel the walls closing in on me. For the moment I needed a temporary escape from the tormenting thoughts of the worse. I'd always found drinking, drugging and sex as my greatest escape from the problems that occurred in my life and although I had no bottle to cradle, I had the woman instead, but this contributed to my being trapped; cornered.

I was awakened by a soft hand gently touching my stomach. "The police is out there!" Denise's frightened voice exclaimed.

"Shit !" I said to myself realizing that I had done it again. As always, after sex with liquor in my system, I would literally pass out. Sometimes I would pass out from excessive drinking period.

I immediately rose to my feet and ran to the living room where there was a little outside light. Peering from the other side of the curtain, I could see uniformed deputies and detectives huddled as though they were making plans for the next football play. After putting the curtain back in place, I focused my attention on Vera and her boyfriend who were seated in the living room on the hideaway bed.

142

Neither of us said word as we made eye contact.

I returned to the back room where Denise was and took her into my arms after nervously lighting a cigarette. I was concerned for her; how I involved her. She was only sixteen living with Vera awaiting her fiancé's release from prison. I disrupted her wait for her fiancé and her lost focus resulted in her heading to prison right along with me. But there was nothing I could do for her, or for me. We could only try to prevent the chains of justice from taking us into custody. But such chances were extremely slim.

"This is what I want you to do," I began my request to Denise. "Go over David and Kati's house to see if anyone is there. If not, break in and open the front door."

David and Kati wouldn't mind me breaking into their house, I believed.

Although displeased with her unsuccess, I took Denise in my arms again realizing that this could be the last time I held a female for a long time, if at all. As I was holding her, a knock came at the door.

"Tell who ever it is, if dey lokin' fo' me, that I'm not here," I told Denise.

"Is Toby here?" Joyce asked after Denise opened the door.

"No, he's not!" Denise exclaimed in a tone that exhibited hate.

When Joyce left the house, I went back into the living room to peer out of the window and saw her get into the car with my family— my aunt, grandmother and grandfather.

There came another knock at the door shortly thereafter. "Denise," I began when seeing her heading towards the door.

"Yea, I know, you ain't here."

"Is there a Toby Williams here?" a detective questioned.

"No," Denise lied. Denise closed the door, but just as she was walking towards the living room another knock came. Vera's boyfriend opened the door.

"Can we come in and have a look around?" The detective questioned.

"I don't know, you have to ask the lady of da house," Vera's boyfriend responded as he pulled the door without closing it all the way.

As soon as he walked away from the door, two detectives came in. When the outside light began to flood the trailer, I immediately ran for cover, finding my way into one of the rooms, trying to hide under the bed. Just as I pulled my leg in under the bed, one of the detectives noticed the movement.

"Here he is in here!" The detectives stormed in raising the bed, forcing me onto my stomach to handcuff me. They began searching me as they held me, finding about three 30-30 Winchester shells in my coat pocket. After they read me my Rights, they place me inside the plain police vehicle while questioning me about the guns. "Where are the guns?" one of the detectives questioned.

"They're in the woods."

"Where in the woods?"

I picked a place out hoping that this would deter them from the trailer where the guns were located.

The detectives stopped at the area of the woods I claimed the guns were. "Show us where they are," one of the detectives ordered.

"They should be over in dis area," I responded, nodding my head into the direction.

After a short search of the area, one of the detectives looked into my direction with hatred in his eyes. "They're not here. We really don't have time for this!" he exclaimed. We stood in silence for a moment, everyone's attention being focused on me.

"Let's go," the detective who was holding my arm said. I was escorted to a police vehicle where two uniformed city police awaited.

A crowd of people gathered down the street in the area we had to go through and in the middle of the crowd, I could see a camera crew from one of the local news stations.

"Nigger, you know what's fixen to happen to you?" one of the police began. "Dey goin' drop that pill on your black ass, you goin' die boy."

I had a vision of blood pouring from parts of my face as I knew in the back of my mind that they would beat me beyond recognition as they had done many prisoners. Death would be preferable to escape the excruciating pain that would be inflicted upon me.

As I sat in the back seat of the police vehicle behind a partition, I could recall when my aunt used to tell me about the beatings the city police would inflict upon the majority of men that would come through the city jail and how the police would sneak the men into a hospital in the middle of the night to get patched up. My time had arrived.

I was too young to comprehend the magnitude of police brutality of the sixties, but my future held the appalling possibility of experiencing a taste of it in the eighties.

Instead of going to the city jail, I was taken to the parish jail in the heart of downtown Shreveport. After we got inside, the city police left me in the custody of the parish deputies. They sat me down in front of a detective.

"Here you are Mr. Williams," the medium built middle aged Caucasian detective stated as he handed me a coke when I seated myself in a chair in front of his desk. "I got him from here," he told the deputies. They put my handcuffs in front.

"Do you smoke Mr. Williams?" he questioned as he closed the door.

Smoke! I smoked like a burning building. With what I was facing, you could include my smoking like a burning forest in the middle of summer.

"Yea," I replied.

"Here you are," he continued as he held the pack of Winston cigarettes toward me with a cigarette partly extended from the pack.

After I took the cigarette in my mouth, the detective flicked his lighter for me to get a light. Winston wasn't my choice of cigarette, but I found the drag long and delightful. This was the only thing, at present, I found pleasure in.

I knew what was ahead. I've experienced it all too many times before. The detective attempted to reveal to me through giving me a coke and cigarettes that he was my friend in order that I would give him information to make his job easier in the investigation on the charges they had against me.

"Mr. Williams," he began. "You have some serious charges here," the detective stated after he was seated and sorted through the documents on his desk.

"Can I get another cigarette?" I requested when I smoked the first one to the butt. He immediately dropped his ink pen to retrieve the pack of cigarettes from his shirt pocket.

I took the butt of the still lit cigarette he gave me earlier to light the second cigarette. I knew he would agree to allow me another cigarette. Matter of fact, he would agree to allow me to smoke the whole pack, which I was determined to do before being placed in a cell without any.

"Look, Mr. Williams," he began. "We can help each other out. I can keep you from getting the electric chair if you will tell me exactly what happened in this case.

"You full of shit," I said to myself. There was nothing he could do for me but continue allowing me to smoke his cigarettes. A few more cokes wouldn't hurt.

After my agreement to provide him with a statement, he immediately retrieved the tape recorder from his desk drawer.

"Today is December 20, 1984," he began speaking into the tape recorder's receiver.

Before going into his line of questioning concerning the criminal episode, he covered some routine questions that would reveal my full name, age, and where I was from.

"Okay, Mr. Williams, you were arrested for multiple charges: Capital murder, attempted capital murder, armed robbery, burglary, three counts of kidnapping and evading arrest. Can you tell me a bit about this and who were involved?"

I went into a fictional narrative about this case in order to prevent the arrest of Vera and Denise although I made admission regarding my involvement. I didn't care because I knew the evidence would be astounding against me, especially by the surviving victim.

The ring of the telephone caused the detective to pause. "I see, okay," he stated.

After he hung up the phone, he walked to the door and gave me a furtive glance. When he opened the door, I noticed Denise and Vera sitting in front of a desk. I was distraught after witnessing the apprehension of my co-defendants. I did all I knew to do with my fictional narrative in order to buy them enough, time to make their escape.

Many questions flooded my head. "What have they done?" "What did they say?" "Did they provide the officials with statements?" "Did they show them where the guns were?"

"Mr. Williams," the detective began, disrupting my thoughts. "Whenever you decide you want to cooperate with us, notify the jailer."

His remarks revealed that he didn't have all the information he wanted me to believe he had from my co-defendants. The only information my co-defendants could provide was what happened that particular night, therefore, he still needed me because it was revealed that my knowledge concerning the case ran deeper where it began with a former acquaintance of Mr. Milholand, one of the victims, who contributed to law enforcement obtaining my name.

As we proceeded into the hall, a large number of people from the media were gathered. My thoughts returned to statements my aunt used to make when witnessing people trying to cover up their face after their apprehension of some hideous crime. Although I had a lot to be ashamed of, the remembrance of my aunt's statement caused me to hold my head up as the cameras focused on me.

After we got into the elevator, I began watching the detectives closely to see if they would make some type of an aggressive move that I was unfamiliar with. Since I wasn't handcuffed any longer, I thought I would have a fighting chance if things resorted to disarray. I was relieved when the elevator arrived at its destination without incident.

Everything and everyone seemed to have passed me by as a result of my incarceration in the boy's home, I considered as I, for the first time in my life, laid in an adults' jail cell.

The wreckage of my life was now lying in a heap in the middle of the interstate, causing traffic jams and impatient motorists in pursuit of obtaining something more out of life then to be held up because of the consequences of my recklessness. I had permitted myself to drive through life without the proper training, training that would have provided me with proper credentials. I had acquired the knowledge of hot wiring my way through life and pushed into driving what was stolen. The wrecker on a few occasions stopped to render aide but there were too many pieces of me lying splattered in the middle of the interstate of life causing him to realize that proper tools were not in his possession. Even the emergency medical crews trained for saving lives could not reach me in time. My life was too much of a bloody mess for anyone to consider resuscitation. Death beckoned, and the chains of justice drew me into its grips.

CHAPTER XXIII

INSANE.

I stared into the wet street as the van traveled from the parish jail to the Caddo Detention Center. It seemed as though I had been in the parish jail for weeks. There was no way to tell whether it was day or night. One could only estimate the time by the meals. I had remained in that cell for a week. The only time anyone was allowed out was for a court appearance, to visit a lawyer or family, a detective or shower.

The Caddo Detention Center was formerly known as the Caddo Correctional Institution. This would be my second trip, but this trip would be for an extended stay. This time I gained an experience I didn't receive the first time.

The first time, I was only twelve years old. I had sat in the car with my grandmother while my aunt and her friend visited her husband.

But now, 7 years later, I would get the experience to live inside the place I once visited.

Due to the nature of my offense, I was placed in the maximum-security section of the prison. Although it was just a holding facility, there were people there under prison sentences living in a designated area. With all the time the gavel of justice would give me, I was sure that I wouldn't be there long before heading to my destination—Angola.

I was housed on the bottom of two rows at the very end of the run, where I lived next door to two men who were brothers. I grew close to one of them. I discovered that he and his brother had been incarcerated before and from his incarcerated education he began to teach me. Although I had serious charges, I had a playful attitude which he pointed out to me that I needed to change. I had to be more serious because I was in for murder, therefore, my peers would have more respect for me and just in case I was faced with confrontation, he started to teach me how to box. We would work out extensively military style; push-ups, sit-ups, throwing to each other a 25lb. medicine bag. On some occasions he would stand over me as I laid on the floor and throw

the bag onto my stomach with force, and while
lying there on my back I was required to throw
the bag upward to him for 5 sets of ten and he
would gradually increase the sets. The more
they increased, the less I would count. I was
simply determined to get through the work
outs because I realized that there was a rough
road ahead. Angola State Penitentiary was my
future, and there, I'd heard, was where they
"play for keeps."

 There was no letting anything slide like in the
boy's home. With my appearance and stature,
someone would definitely try me. It would
have to result in a fight to the bloody end. With
the kind of time the gavel of justice would
throw at me, I would definitely have to commit
murder, again, because there's no such thing as
although he don't know how to fight, but he'll
fight. There's no such thing as a loss or a tie.
That would lead to more fights and more
people who would attempt to break me.

I would stand before my neighbor throwing
my fist, learning the best boxing techniques,
but the technique I was in dire need of was
knife fighting —becoming a notorious
murderer.

My neighbor and I would work out and hang
out with each other on a regular basis. We
were allowed an hour in the morning and two
hours in the afternoon for recreation in the
dayroom or outside in the recreation yard.
During the evening recreation time, we were
only allowed an hour in the dayroom, but on
one particular morning my door didn't open
for recreation. I thought that there was a
malfunction in the door but I discovered that I
was considered too dangerous to recreate and
be in contact with other people due to the
nature of the offense. The officials had started
to handcuff and shackle me to simply walk
down the hall in the maximum security wing
where I was housed. They had got to the point
where they were handcuffing and shackling
me to visit my family behind a partition. This
had gone to far, "I've had enough of this shit !"
I thought.

My neighbor had informed me that, according
to the news clippings he'd seen of me on
television, I had a look as though I was
unaware of what was going on. The making of
an insanity plea was birthed. The officials
already believed that I was insane. Everything
the news media would show and write about
me had insane implications. Insanity was

exactly what they would get out of me. Along with the media's report, my past psych experience and some good acting for the purpose of documentation, I would definitely have an insanity plea.

My neighbor assisted me with my first scene and gathered up some extras—other men— to give the scene some flavor, some texture.

Act one began with a roll of toilet paper and some matches. I unrolled some of the paper in the middle of the floor in between my legs as I sat on the bunk. My neighbor had told me that if I started a fire, they would be required to open my door. Once I notified him that I was ready, he and some of the other men got the attention of the officer.

As I awaited his arrival I entered a chant, similar to one speaking in tongues, in order that I may be in an award-winning, insane, character upon his arrival. When I noticed him from my peripheral vision, I set the fire.

Although I continued in my chanting, in my mind I was saying: "Ooh, man, this fire sure is hot! I almost ceased what I was doing because of the fire, but he said something, and I was able to use it as a que to escape the fire. Although the cell door was closed, I faced the officer standing at attention like a soldier in the military.

"What are you doing? He questioned.

In my mind I was thinking, "What the hell you think I'm doing? all this fire in here."

He stepped away from the door to order the officer controlling to doors, to open the cell door.

"Come on out!" he instructed.

At this time, I had no clue as to what I was about to do. From this point on I would have to improvise. I had failed to think this thing through.

When I stepped out of the cell and turned to the direction I would be going, I heard, "run!" I don't know if it was one of my neighbors or if it was just a voice in my head, but I said to myself. "That's a good idea." So I took off running. On the other end were about five officers who simply watched me. The officer controlling the doors stepped out and closed the gate on me. I was too close to make a stop, I hadn't anticipated this. I made a jump and when I landed on the bars, I was hurt. But I had come to far to turn back now. I began to growl like a dog as the officer looked at me with fear in his eyes. Then all of a sudden officers began to wrestle me from the bars, onto the floor. When they had me on the floor, I bit one of them. When he began to holler and scream that I had bit him the other officers quickly released me. I was so tired that I simply laid in the floor to allow them to handcuff me.

When one of the ranking officers came in to talk to me, I simply asked him, "Man, what's up? Why y'all got me in here ?"

"You been acting up."

"I ain't don' nothin'."

About an hour later I was allowed to return to my cell with about seven escorts where I would prepare for my next scene, but I was never allowed to due to the State of Texas seeking me for prosecution.

CHAPTER XXIV

TEXAS BOUND.

The monitoring screen had revealed that my plan was in good health but there came complications in the birth process that took me into the intensive care unit to reveal my future in a broken-down Texas legal system that desired to place me on a faulty life support system with judicial intentions of pulling the plug.

I had fought extradition by refusing to sign extradition documents that would permit the Texas officials to take me into custody for prosecution, but my fight was to no avail. I was now Texas bound, and they wanted all of me—until death do us part!

Upon my arrival in Texas, I went before a magistrate judge who read me my Miranda rights and asked if I would sign. "No!" was my flat reply. I had already given them too much when I fail weak in signing an incriminating statement when the Texas law enforcement visited me in Louisiana. I had hoped that my affixed signature would have some type of impact that would get some of the charges reduced. I had at the time believed that my codefendants had signed statements, "what could mine hurt," I thought. I had done what I knew to do to help them escape apprehension by lying to the Louisiana law enforcement officials about two other people being involved. Many documents had been placed before me by different people. "Read this!" "Sign this!" It would appear that I was in an executive position where secretaries and paralegals were seeking my signature in order to process my documentative desires. My position was definitely not of an officiating position, but it was official that I was in the arms of incarceration once again, on my way to prison, this time—to have a date with death!

I had never considered being sentenced to death and wasn't aware of the procedures that would render such a fate, but I discovered through the media's report that Texas was seeking the death penalty against me.

It wouldn't have made a difference what they had in mind to do now, it was all over for me.

I could dismiss thoughts of being a father because I had lost my son. I could dismiss the plans I had to be a husband because I had lost my future wife, or to holding on to my lover because she was in jail with me. There was no concern now for having my own home or car, or having accomplished my own jail cell where the walls would play the many horrific tuneless songs of nights passed to incapacitate my thoughts and send my body into animalistic rage. My present situation was unbearable, and I was forced to sit in what I considered a western day jail surrounded by my thoughts, walls and bars. Alone had left me with no one to fight but my thoughts, no one to lean on but the walls, no one to look at but the bars. "I can't suffer no more than this, I have nothing to lose!"

BAM! BAM! BAM! my kicks were enraged with violence on the steel door. The slap of my mother's abandonment was in my kick. The cut of my father's neglect and death, the fist of my stepbrothers pounding into me and their ridiculing attitudes, all those who jumped on me was in my kick. The psychological and verbal abuse of my step family saying I would never be nothing and end up in prison. All the boys that pursued me sexually, my anger for being arrested, for all that I lost was in my kick. My hate, loneliness, all the anger, bitterness and grief I could muster was in my kick.

All the detectives, deputies and jailers that ran to put out the fire of my kicks were in my kicks.

One out of about nine men that ran to the scene came to the door to give me a direct order to cease what I was doing, but I was beyond being ordered. I wanted to hurt someone and had no concern that that someone was me in hopes that it would allow me to escape the bitter torture that was raging in my soul.

"Y'all get me the fuck out of here!" I yelled with a growl in my voice as my mouth foamed like a dog with rabies as tears streamed down my face.

I had tried the dramatizing acting career of insanity that could possibly have prevented me from experiencing the harsh consequences of my crimes or cause charges I was facing to be reduced, but I was not playing a role anymore. I had slipped into the asylum of insanity. I had lost control.

However, this rage subsided and within 3 days they released me from their jail. I would be transferred to the Marshall, Texas.

CHAPTER XXV

BACKYARD FRIENDS.

Crawling around in the dirt in my aunt's
backyard with my toys was where I often
visited my feelings; my hurts, my cries that
were locked away in the dungeon of my being
like caged animals that would tearfully scream
down my face. I was about ten or eleven. But
there to my rescue were my imaginary friends.
Yes, you know them. They are the ones who
will be there in the time of need, the ones who
will cry with you when you need to cry, who
will laugh with you when you need to laugh,
who will listen to you when you need to talk ,
who will talk to you when you need to listen.
They are the friends you can trust, the friends
you can count on, who wouldn't gossip behind
your back or leave you stranded in the
trenches of difficulty. It doesn't matter if
you're angry, agitated, or aggravated; it doesn't
matter if you're deaf, dumb, or deranged, if

you're weak, reckless, or worried; they will be there. In the lowest state of being, they faithfully stand by your side.

The animals —dogs and cats— who were present would watch me from a distance. Although we had no way to verbally communicate, I often believed that they could hear the screams of torment within me as they wouldn't come around me until I called them and then would come running with playful attitudes. They were the only ones I could put my arms around and feel comforted by. The only ones I didn't have to worry about becoming abusive toward me or ridicule me because I didn't know how to formulate a sentence, or because I was a failure at everything, but they were not allowed to be with me in my present situation.

I had been transferred from Marshall to Rusk State Mental hospital where I was given a battery of tests and asked many questions by psychiatrists, psychologists, counselors, and physicians.

I had been through it all before where psychiatrists, psychologists, counselors, and physicians tried to probe the contours of my mind to make an analysis of what caused me to malfunction.

I was thirteen years old when my aunt admitted herself into a mental health facility for evaluation for the purpose of seeing if she was fit to continue raising me. She was released in good mental health and instructed to bring me in for evaluation.

I was given a battery of tests in the mental health facility and asked many questions about my experiences and how I felt about them. I primarily shared some of what I'd endured with my mother, father and step family. I

I didn't go into much detail about my experiences. I didn't know these people, besides, there was nothing they could do for me, I considered. Therefore, they were really a waste of my time as they never revealed whether or not my mental capacity was in question. Eventually I stopped going. "I quit!" I told myself.

I had quickly grown out of my toys and deeper into my cigarettes, liquor, and marijuana. All the help I needed was in them. When I needed to tell a young lady something romantic, my help was in them, or when I needed to express something serious to someone. If I needed a psychiatrist, psychologist, counselor, or physician, I could, find in cigarettes, dope and alcohol.

To find me mentally incapacitated, these doctors would merely prescribe for me some type of mind altering drug. I was content with the mind altering drugs I prescribed for myself.

I had discovered that once anyone quit they weren't allowed to return but I was considered a special case.

Although the mental health facility never revealed to me their prognosis, the records they maintained in their file would assist me years later.

But now I was under a new panel of doctors in Rusk Mental hospital who were trying to establish whether I was competent to stand trial. They would ask me such questions as what was the purpose of a judge, prosecutor, and defense attorney. What was my crime and the consequences, after asking me routine questions about my name, where I was from, and where I lived. According to law in connection' with the offense capital murder, I was insane until proven sane. I was incompetent until proven competent.

I had been required to do little drawings, look at pictures to observe what was in them and put blocks in a certain form. I always felt like I was in some type of kindergarten class. I put forth my best failing effort. I didn't have the aid of my self-prescribed drugs. I had wondered if I was mentally incapacitated in some way since I couldn't stay out of the arms of incarceration but came to the conclusion that I would be jeopardizing insanity and incompetence.

Since the law established me being insane and incompetent for the offense I committed, I needed to remain in accordance to what the law established or else the gavel of justice would surely sentence me to death because there was too much evidence against me to expect receiving anything less.

My desire to be considered mentally incapacitated was crushed when I discovered within a week that I was being transferred back to the Marshall jail. I don't know where I failed to cause them to find me competent; to find me sane, but I couldn't afford to be such. I had no master plan as to how I could accomplish reversing this decision, but something needed to happen because my doom was fast approaching. Court dates were now scheduled.

CHAPTER XXVI

COURT IS NOW IN SESSION.

There's an old cliché which says to hope for the best but expect the worst. This is primarily for the purpose of preparing oneself to receive the worst because one has basically lost hope.

 Court was in session and I knew that

Hell awaited my arrival.

Due to the large amount of publicity surrounding my case in the East Texas area, I had been transferred to McKinney, Texas for the purpose of trial after the judicial officials granted me a change of venue.

Twelve jurors and one alternate juror were picked from a panel of about 100-125 potentials. They would decide my fate by the evidence laid before them by the prosecuting attorney who bared the burden of proving that I was the perpetrator of capital murder as charged in the indictment. Under a separate indictment I was charged with attempted capital murder and these were both being tried simultaneously. Although the prosecutor was required to prove the case to the jury for the purpose of them returning a guilty verdict, the expression on their faces appeared to announce me guilty after the reading of the indictments.

"The deck is stacked against me," I thought. "I'm broke, black and on trial for murder." The law established that I'm innocent until proven guilty, but I was sure that this jury had me guilty until proven innocent.

I hardly gave any attention to the proceedings and had no concern if they stopped the proceeding to carry out my execution. My appearance in court was merely formality. The first day was of interest though. My co-defendant, Vera, testified against me. Her testimony described the night in question. She testified that we approached the victim's residence armed with a .357 magnum and ordered him back inside after he came out of the house. She also testified that I had Mr. *victim* to assist me by putting his property on his truck and how I left for the purpose of withdrawing his money from his savings account. The portion of the testimony that held all on the edge of their seats was her description of, the actual murder. Vera tearfully described that we drove the Victims across the state line into Texas where I ordered Mr. *victim* and his wife out of the car and fired a single shot from a 30-30 rifle that went into the back of his wife through to end up in his abdomen .

My state appointed attorney pursued to cross examine her in order to reveal to the court that she was lying but he was unsuccessful.

 Although I had lost hope for myself, I hoped that her testimony would assist her to receive less than what she bargained for, but it was established between her and the judicial authorities that she would receive a life sentence for her testimony against me.

I wasn't upset with her in the least for what she decided to do. As a matter of fact, I encouraged it. I had the opportunity to spend a day talking to her in the Carthage jail where a part of our discussion was about her testifying against me. I had the opportunity to see and speak with both Denise and Vera on a regular basis while in the Marshall jail since we were housed across the hall from each other when I was in the population tank. Occasionally an officer would leave the men and women beam slots opened. I had expressed to Denise that she could testify against me if she so chose, but she declined. She received forty years for her admittance in the crime.

The victim testified that our acquaintance was beyond the night in question. I used to work for him. I was merely an extra hand to assist the opening of a recreational vehicle business. He also testified that the bullet ended up in his abdomen.

A Louisiana official testified that my palm print was lifted from the murder weapon and that a fingerprint of mine was lifted from the victim's Buick.

My attorney was successful in preventing the autopsy from being introduced in court since the coroner was not present to testify concerning it. The prosecutor tried to admit it after a magistrate judge revealed his opinion of the cause of death. Despite the absence of the coroner's testimony and report,

I was convicted of capital murder.

Although I braced myself for this conclusion, the impact jolted my calloused attitude and scattered my thoughts. It was definitely over. The only two sentences available were life or death.

Upon entering into the punishment phase of the trial, the stares of the jurors were cold and piercing as they appeared to announce—*death!*

The first witness was a great surprise. It was five years prior that I saw the fear in his eyes as he sat on the ground as I pointed the .22 revolver at his face in order to eliminate my only witness. Although he was not allowed to testify against me when I was a juvenile, he was on my adult trial to give testimony to persuade the jury to render a sentence of death.

He testified that I shot him, but I wondered if he knew that my intentions were to kill him.

The prosecution was required to show that I was a continuing threat to society. The basis of his evidence would determine whether or not the jury would access death.

CHAPTER XXVII

DEATH ROW!

Prison's poison had been spun in the cylinder of incarcerations' revolving door. At the pull of the trigger of my adult criminal interest, the poison contributed to chambering me into the abyss of prison experience, stripping away my life in freedom's light to lay me on the slab of a cold morgue after cutting away the organs of importance and tagging me with a prison number.

The dirt of prison life was shoveled upon me, to bury me just below isolation, where my bones would wax cold—beyond the fading memory of those who once considered my existence in freedom's light.

Here is where the weeds of negativity grow and dismantle any effort to pursue anything positive. Here you'll hear the excruciating, horrifying sound of mutilation thunder out of the heart of the angry, agitated and aggravated.

Here you'll witness misery finding companionship and establishing immoral relationships beyond imagination.

Here you'll find hostility raining in the lives of those who were humble, to wet them with the storm of hate.

Morality becomes marred and principles are abandoned. The pitfalls of the past paralyze to prevent any aspiration to achieve anything accessible.

 Here is where animosity protrudes the morbid corridors of the trifling in pursuit of dirtying the floors of the resourceful. Here is where the secrets of the past creep into one's presence, to lurk in the far dark corners of their being, to stir up strife.

 Life is purchased for coffee and cigarettes;

Where an individual could be bought for as little as ten dollars. The rejected and dejected are subjected to serve as *unwilling prison slaves*.

Here stress and strain often visit to slit a wrist, a throat and hang one from a noose; where arrogance runs rampart to belittle the less fortunate. The battle for intelligence is lost to ignorance.

Here is where the stone of procrastination lays hopelessly with laziness; where gossip, lies and rumors reign supreme.

Here is where the worms of trauma crawl insidiously to eat away at dignity. Where the smoke of abuse rises to choke the beast into a state of rage.

The fire of insult vehemently burns to leave the scar of humiliation.

Here is where the many broken, fractured and wounded hearts abide; polluted through circumstances that locked, barred and bolted them behind the stone door of the tomb. Here the pimps are played, the players are pushed, and the pushers are pimped.

The venomous poison of the past often seeps out in conversations and actions of the condemned as it is expressed and revealed how many, as children, experienced being chained, bound and beaten by their own parents, relatives or people they trusted. Beaten with chains and water hoses and dragged in the middle of the street.

Some parents, relatives and people they
trusted, molested and- forced many of them to
have sex with *animals* and other people, and
there are some who had been cut, stabbed and
shot by parents, relatives or those they trusted;

Sexually penetrated with broom and mop
handles and other foreign objects that ruptured
their anuses and tore internal tissues and
ruptured internal organs, leaving them for
dead or hospitalized.

Many voices of the tortured and condemned
rage in the night, hurling threats of taking lives
when the opportunity presents itself.

There's the tumultuous cursing-out of someone
to relieve the stress and strain of the
anticipation of execution and the discussion of
those cast into the outer darkness of execution,
often echo in the cry of the night;

The place where pillows burn with hot tears
and mute, muffled cries; the place where
eternal sleep is sought with rigor to escape the
wretched screams of the past and present.

Suicides, attempted suicides and self-
mutilation are all rampant. The condemned
cutting on themselves, hanging themselves and
burning themselves, purposely overdosing on

drugs. The stench of dried blood travels through the housing area to protrude from the nostrils of those in pursuit of holding on to their sanity.

From a dark cell, in the calm of the night, blood streamed from one of the men condemned to die. Further investigation revealed that blood also covered ceiling and walls of his cell.

He had struggled with being possessed by a woman and on this particular night he pursued the need to free her by *castrating himself.*

Ironically, a female officer was to discover him.

Another condemned man would go into hysterical laughter while describing how he obeyed a voice that told him to walk through the blazing fire he set in his cell.

He also described how he would scream when the doctors and nurses would touch him, which aggravated the pain, in order that they could put him into a tub to wash him.

An African-American man who spoke with a thick country accent ingested other people's prescription drugs, which was his way of escaping the psychological torture of death row. One day torture and his drug abuse spiraled into his attempt to commit suicide. He cut his own throat!

A few condemned men that were fed up with living exhausted their appeals as a form of institutional suicide to escape the psychological torture of death row.

Many are the most horrific murder descriptions, which travel the razor wire confines through the conversations of some of the condemned, describing the moans, cries and pleas of their victims, begging for life to the bitter end.

 Some had ended in blood, guts and brains being splattered all over the walls, ceilings, floors, and furniture from shotgun blasts.

Some used butchers' knives to decapitate and remove limbs from plundered bodies.

Bodies burned and body parts eaten and cut up into small pieces and discarded in different locations.

Strangulations that popped eyes out of their sockets.

Strangulations while committing rape.

The descriptions of tongues getting cut out of the victim's mouth and throats sliced like some kind of fruit.

And there are those who commit necrophilia and cut out their victims' genitals.

There are those who experience orgasm as they repeatedly stab their victim without abandon. Techniques that rip and tear flesh and break bones.

Blunt objects used to crush skulls. Foreign objects used to penetrate and rip apart anuses and sexual organs.

Those whose bodies are thrown in a bath tub of acid. Some of the descriptions are of bodies buried in cement, buried in ponds, rivers, lakes, seas and oceans.

Murder and attempted murder often occur. One particular man had been stabbed on a couple occasions, had a homemade bomb thrown in his cell that resulted in third degree burns all over his body. He was finally murdered by another condemned man who strangled him to death with a jump rope during recreation.

Another condemned was murdered with a
porkchop bone as officers stood by and
watched in horror.

The stench of this hell beckons those who are
in possession of a Russian-Roulette mentality.
The mentality that sends its participant out
into the dark of night for the purpose of easing
the pain of the past with violence or for the
purpose of making that next hustle, turn fatal,
to capitalize on someone's earnings in order to
feed a habit or fulfill some type of lustful
desire.

Here is where the mummified dead abode,
wrapped in the bitter torture of the past and
present and here is where the dead will
welcome your arrival —here is...

DEATH ROW!

CHAPTER XXVIII

JUMP STREET 21.

The winter's bitter cold constantly swept through the broken windows of the wing in which the maintenance shop purposely failed to repair. They realized that they would be broken immediately after repair as had occurred on many occasions.

The year was 1986, the same year I was approved through the unit's classification to go to the work program where I was allowed a cell partner and worked in the garment factory. However, an incident with an officer resulted in my receiving a disciplinary infraction for Refusing to Obey an Order, resulting in my removal from the work program. He had told me to go to my cell belligerently, my response:

"Put me in my damn cell then!"

He grabbed my arm and I jerked it from his hand. Since he put his hands on me he was required to write the infraction to cover himself after discovering that I had filed a Use of Force claim on him. Otherwise, it would have been considered assault. My punishment consisted of 30 days in my cell, commissary restriction and removal from the work program.

I was moved to wing number J-21, which earned the name Jump Street 21 (in relation to the television episode "21 Jump Street") due to constant occurrences such as: trash and clothes being thrown out into the middle of the run where fires were often started. Although this was a lock down wing, there were many fights and stabbings that has included officers being stabbed by inmates.

This is the wing where the man had been fatally stabbed with a pork chop bone.

Officers and inmates alike experienced having urine and feces being thrown on them. I had witnessed an officer having feces thrown on him by my next door neighbor who everyone referred to as Midnight in regards to his very dark complexion. Midnight was militant and believed in "staying down" for his people, and the officers no matter their race were considered the enemy or "the white man." In the back of his cell he stored feces for weeks in the event an officer offended him or his black brothers. Another condemned man who was African-American experienced a problem with the bed sheet the African-American officer had given him. The officer made a sarcastic remark which alerted Midnight to respond, then the officer made a sarcastic remark toward Midnight and thereafter, Midnight vowed that when the officer return he would have something for him.

Midnight kept his promise. SPLASH!, right in the face.

The officer took it as though he was used to it as some of the feces' particles dribbled out of his mouth.

His facial expression showed no sign of disappointment that the feces tasted bad.

"Man, shit!" I had never witnessed such a sickening sight. The smell was so bad that it effected the whole wing of approximately sixty-eight men who were complaining of the foul odor.

The slamming of cell doors often echoed with volcanic thunder and the sliding of a shield on a rail would give anyone the impression they were living near a railroad. An officer was required to walk in front and one behind the inmate as the inmate walked in front of the sliding shield for protection purposes.

Although the bars were covered with steel mesh, many men have been stabbed as they walked by a cell. There was also fence-like mesh, approximately 2 to 3 feet from the cell doors. Anytime we left our cells we were required to be handcuffed and relieved of them upon reaching our destination. Any wing outside the work program, we were handcuffed when we exited the cell.

Three groups were allowed three-hour recreation periods inside a boxed-in fence. One group in the morning, one in the afternoon and another one in the evening. Our times would rotate. We were allowed to watch television, and play table games such as chess, checkers, and scrabble. Our outside activities included basketball, handball and horseshoes.

I spent a great deal of time pacing the floor of my cell wearing extra clothing to keep warm as I would often talk with the people out of my past. I had the courage to tell them what I couldn't tell them face to face. I could tell my aunt how irritating it was to hear her argue and fuss and carry on conversation I had no interest in hearing. I could tell my mother and father how pathetic I thought they were. I could curse out my step brothers or anybody else I felt I could handle a good cursing. They were not there to hear what I had to say, therefore, I could invent the response I desired. I would also rehearse my lines in the event I'm given another opportunity to enter the courtroom; to primarily tell them about how I felt about the death penalty with its cruelty/or how it is a failure to deter.

One particular night when tempers began to flare up, Midnight and another young man. living opposite me began to argue. The young man would never come out for recreation because his interest was to be in a singleman recreation group but he, out of the argument, decided that he would meet Midnight in the dayroom to fight. I had determined that I wouldn't go out the next morning, but as there was going to be a fight, I couldn't miss having a ring side seat.

Well, instead of watching a fight, I became the participant. Although I knew the story concerning the young man, I disregarded it due to my desire to watch a fight. He was known for striking people with his fist while they were in handcuffs, but on this particular morning, he waited for the officer to release me from the handcuffs. He approached me in a fighting stance and when he got closer, without a word, he took his swing. I was able to block it followed by a jab to keep him off of me long enough to get my socks off because they were causing me to slide, but the ranking officer asked us to stop. I stopped in order that they wouldn't take unnecessary disciplinary action against me, besides, the guy didn't know how to fight. I guess that's why he always waited to jump people handcuffed behind their back. He was merely using these tactics to assist him in getting into the single man recreation group. Although disciplinary action was taken against me, it was only a verbal reprimand.

Many nights, caged behind steel bars and mesh, found my pillow burning with hot tears and mute muffled cries. I considered my life to be over. I had made the ultimate mistake that resulted in the ultimate punishment, *DEATH*! All my memories, what little I had, could now be cast into the lake of fire to eternally burn as was my destination..

CHAPTER XXIX

LEGITIMATE HUSTLE.

Wallowing in the pity of my situation, it seemed that the whole world abandoned me as I sat on death row. It was 1987.

After approximately 4-6 months on J-21, I was returned to the wing that I went to when I arrived on death row. The only difference on this wing was that it did not include steel mesh on the bars and fence-like mesh from the ceiling to the floor. There were no sliding shield, excessive noises, fires and trashed out walkways. For a period of time the wing was extremely noisy because the televisions, mounted on the wall adjacent to our cells for viewing, volume level was blaring in order that we could hear them. There were about twelve of them. Later the administration had the television sound connected to the wall speaker and they provided us with headphones which attributed to the wing being unusually quiet.

I was allowed to return to the work program a few months thereafter where I had entered a legitimate hustle.

My aunt, the only someone sticking by me had disappeared. I was depending on her to help me financially as she had done most of my life. The prison provided three meals a day but most of them were unpleasant, therefore, I desired to purchase my own through the unit's commissary. The prison also provided soap that's primarily good for washing clothes and toothpowder that affects the teethes enamel. At the time I was out of cigarettes and I owed someone a can of tobacco they had loaned me.

There were no places of businesses to rob and no houses to burglarize, and it wouldn't pay to steal from anyone. We were all in the same predicament. I realized that I had to do something but I knew nothing. There were men drawing for profit, but I didn't know how to draw. I could trace, but I didn't know how to mix the colors to color my tracing or shade. I witnessed men making different types of wood projects out of match sticks, but it appeared to be complicated. Oh, well, I have nothing better to do, I could seek to learn, besides, I wasn't accomplishing any financial support through watching television, playing basketball or handball, or playing table games.

I discovered more about how much another mans' trash can be another mans' treasure. One of the men threw away some incomplete wood projects: a jewelry box and a couple of wooden crosses. I gave the jewelry box to Ben, whom I befriended; he made jewelry boxes. Ben had promised to teach me the craft once he completed the project he was working on for his mother.

Match sticks were required to make these projects, but I had none, therefore, I asked different people to save their match sticks for me. I had made the man, responsible for cleaning up, aware that he don't have to worry about sweeping the dayroom any more, "I got it," I told him.

"Toby, what are you doing?" I remember one of the men asking.

"I'm getting this money out of here." After sweeping the dayroom I would dig the match sticks out of the trash pile, take them to my cell to cut off the burnt portion in order to artistically glue them on the cross I was completing. Ben had provided me with some glue, sandpaper, a razor blade and razor blade holder he handmade and he gave me a few instructions.

After about three months I received a letter from my aunt making me aware that my grandfather died, which left her to have to pay a percentage for my grandfather's burial due to some bad insurance. I didn't get to know my grandfather well. I met him when I was thirteen or fourteen. My aunt had brought him from Arkansas when she learned that his health was failing in relation to his alcoholism. The most I knew about him is that he loved to rise early in the morning and help with the building on my aunt's house. Often times I would join him and this provided me with the opportunity to learn about building. The experience paid off with regards to my wood projects. Making these projects weren't as complicated as I thought when reflecting on what I learned from my grandfather.

With the news of my grandfather, my aunt sent me 20 dollars. Instead of spending it on commissary, I invested it for some supplies in order that I can make my own money.

I learned that I could either hold my hand out and hope someone would fulfill my wants and needs, or I could put my hands to work to fulfill my own wants and needs. Eventually people get tired of the same old hands being held out that refuse to establish a legitimate hustle.

The time I invested in making the cross turned into $210.00. Although it was a poor job, I sent it to a woman who knew me when I was a boy. She had contacted me just before I began working on the cross. She had given the cross to the church who raised the money for me. I invested about $100.00 in order to take my new craft further. I eventually started ordering clocks to mount on my work. I never sold any of my work but after acquiring a few overseas friends through Amnesty International, I would ask them to send me some financial support for postage in order to send them what I had made. The majority of times they would send me more then what my project was worth, therefore, I was content with that. I had also started making jewelry boxes and picture frames. And I would send my aunt and son" and the lady who helped me, some of my handmade projects.

Although my aunt eventually resumed sending me financial support, I didn't have to depend on her for it. I began to learn more about responsibility, creativity and management. Sometimes that which appears to be a set-back is a blessing in disguise.

Although I was able to take care of my debt, the ultimate debt was nearing;

I was to pay with my very life.

CHAPTER XXX

NO-NAMED GRAVE.

The news I received was inevitable. I had learned in 1988 that the appeals court had denied my appeal. The problem associated with the news was that it was a former Dallas police officer who relayed it. He lived next door to me on death row.

"Toby, you want me to write the death row clinic for you?" he questioned.

"Do what?"

"Oh, you don't know?"

"Know what?"

He handed me an open book as he pointed to my name, revealing that the appeals court denied my case. I was more concerned about why my attorney failed to relay this message to me.

Although my attorney failed to contact me, it wasn't until November, 1991 that an officer came to my cell to inform me that I would be bench warranted back to Panola County. Under these circumstances, a court will bench warrant the individual immediately. It's purpose: to announce the date of the individual's execution.

The sentence does not become final until after the appeals court affirm. And although the appeals court affirmed and an individual received the first execution date, it is not considered dangerous unless an attorney fails to meet the deadline for filing an appeal without providing the individual notice of his failure. The first execution date normally forces an attorney to go forward with the next step, the appeal process. Should a lawyer fail to meet the deadline, it has the potential to entail fatal consequences.

My heart pounded with rapid tempo as I entered the cold courtroom. The person I desired not to be present was there—my aunt. I didn't want her to witness what was about to transpire.

Once again, I stood before the judge who announced my sentence. And once again, he asked me to stand. He announced my execution date for March 20, 1992. He thereafter had the audacity to ask me if I had something to say. Of course, I had something to say. I had prepared for this moment during the many nights I paced my death row cell to rehearse my lines, but for the first time in my life I was staring in the face of death. I forgot! I felt like I was going to pass out as I felt a numbness in the back of my neck. I was finally able to mumble something even I couldn't understand. My trial attorney sought to come to my rescue. "What did you say?""

His voice seemed to be distant although he was right next to me. "Not at this time," I was finally able to say and hurriedly returned to my seat.

The letter the former police wrote for me assisted me to acquire approximately 6-7 attorneys from one of the most prestigious law firms in the State of Texas, Baker & Botts. The leading attorney from the firm argued in her effort to convince the judge to overturn his decision, to no avail.

The evidence established that my aunt was distraught. In our visit afterward, she stated, with tears in the well of her eyes, "If I don't see you again on this side, maybe I'll see you on the other side."

Upon my return to Ellis unit, I sought to keep my execution date a secret. Nevertheless, it became public knowledge.

On March, 19, 1992, I was instructed at approximately 0600 hours to move to the death watch cell where every thirty minutes an officer logged in a special death watch report about what he or she witnessed me doing. I sought to appear unaffected, but I felt crushed, and confused. My nerves were beyond being on edge. I had thought I was brave, I never feared dying, but it's something about staring death in the face that makes a difference.

As I paced the floor, another condemned prisoner spoke to me through a small window of the dayroom. To him I tried to appear strong and unaffected, but deep within I believed my predicament was evident. I believe he knew I wanted to crawl in a corner to allow the tears to stream down my face. I believe he knew that I wanted to fall apart in order to cease shaking, which was obvious in my voice, "This surely can't be it!" I told myself. "Have you heard anything?" I questioned an officer monitoring me.

"No!" his voice sarcastically thundered a response. Perhaps it was merely magnified in relation to my predicament.

I had endured many things in life, but they were now of no concern, they were now unimportant.

Some of what I endured would accompany me to the grave.

I could only hope that my first execution date would not find me strapped and bound with leather belts on the Texas gurney of death where a saline solution would be injected in my veins before the lethal injection would be given.

I couldn't imagine what was going through my aunt's mind who would be required to claim my body. Perhaps my death would be too unbearable for her that would have caused her to leave my body unclaimed and left for the prison to bury me in a box built by other inmates. My execution number, 000806, would have been my only identification on a cross that would also bear the year of my burial.

For many years I contemplated dying. I had even entertained the thought of committing "institutional suicide" by exhausting my appeals and allowing the State to execute me. But now fear struck, leaving me wondering whether or not I was going to something better. Will death take me away from my living nightmare, or will I fall into the abyss of a nightmare far worse than the one I was experiencing?

The desire I had to leave this world quietly could be accomplished, I had thought. Death waits for no one.

It had been said that the life we live on earth determines our eternal life. Taking that into consideration, I had nothing much to expect. I could only hope that misery does not exist there. I could only hope that the trials, traumas and tribulation of life only exist on Earth. In that moment I was allowed to see more clearly; how there's more to life than seeking drugs, alcohol and sex. There's more to life than seeking material things. There's more to life than just existing, than pursuing to live up to someone else's expectation.

It has been said that a person is not ready to live until they are prepared to die. I had never been prepared, I was just ready, ready because I was too much of a coward to desire pressing on in spite of what I endured, ready because it

202

appeared that I didn't matter. Since I was merely ready to die, my attitude towards death exemplified the fact that I was not at all prepared to die   I guess that's why I never lived. As I peered in the face of death, I entered the realization that was not ready, but..

DEATH WAITS FOR NO ONE!

CHAPTER XXXI

STAY OF EXECUTION.

While I was pacing the floor of the death watch cell, an officer had finally come by to make me aware of my stay of execution. I was very confused under the circumstances because the day before my move to the death watch cell, I had discovered through a telephone conversation with one of my lawyers that I had received a stay of execution. One minute there was the mentioning of receiving a stay of execution and the next moving to a death watch cell. Although I was a bit shaken up as I stared in the face of death, I was sure that my attorneys would straighten everything out. I discovered later that their failure to do so could lead to my execution.

In June of 1992, I had received a federal express letter from one of my attorneys concerning the response they received regarding my postconviction writ. I sat the package aside momentarily because I was afraid to open it to find unpleasant news, but my curiosity convinced me to open it. Upon my glance at the letter, my eye caught,

"I'm pleased to..." I realized that it had to be some good news, so I focused my attention on the content of the letter and discovered that the Court of Criminal Appeals had vacated (overturned) my conviction regarding mitigating circumstances. The court forbade the jury from considering my mental capacity. The Rusk State hospital had concluded that I was mildly mentally retarded based on my test scores. The records from the Shreveport mental facility supported the findings. In spite of the findings, unpleasant news could possibly be in the future, I realized, since the prosecutor had fifteen days from the time of the ruling to request the Court of Criminal Appeals to reinstate the death penalty. Later, I discovered that the prosecutor decided not to challenge the ruling any further than the Court of Criminal Appeals. The prosecutor thereafter requested a bench warrant for me to return to the county jail; an unusual request for a prosecutor.

My return to Panola County was filled with optimism; the course of history was on the verge of unfurling a new direction during the presidential elections. During the process, the Panola County District Attorney, watched with great anticipation, hoping that the Democratic Party, Arkansas Governor, William Jefferson Clinton, would experience success. Governor Clinton's success would play an important role toward his decision to decline seeking the death penalty in my case.

I also watched with great anticipation. I had previously learned through my trial attorney that my success, to escape returning' to death row, hinged on the success of Governor Clinton's Presidential election to become the forty-second President of the United States of America.

In the month of November of 1992, I discovered that the new district attorney was offering me a life sentence. I would accept as long as it wasn't a capital life sentence which makes the sentence aggravated. Under the circumstances, aggravated would take longer to come up for parole, meaning that I would have to accomplish twenty years flat before parole consideration, but that was all he was offering. I expressed to my attorneys that I would prefer to be dead then to plead guilty to a capital life sentence where I would be required to do twelve more years for a total of twenty years. Of course I wasn't staring death in the face and felt brave again. I constantly thought about it and eventually told my aunt about it but she seemed to be a bit discouraged that I hadn't accepted and thereafter relayed to me that my stay on death row had caused her some problems, something I had been causing her all my life. I figured that it was time to draw the line. My desire was to take the case back to trial because I felt that I had a chance to receive a lesser sentence since my trial attorney was more familiar with the case and I had the assistance of other attorneys, including my increased knowledge of the law. Yes, I was considering gambling with my life when in fact I had been given a break, which is something a death row inmate rarely receives, especially in Texas.

After all, I could take the case back to trial and wind up with another death sentence and I could spend that twelve years waiting to be executed instead of twelve years to be considered for parole.

I had a scheduled appearance in court to take the capital life sentence, but the scheduled proceeding was cancelled. My trial attorney told me that it looked as though I would receive what I wanted which consisted of a life sentence for 1st degree murder. The prosecutor, judge and my trial attorney discovered that a charge of capital murder would have to be reduced to 1st degree murder in order for a plea agreement to be accomplished, otherwise, a plea agreement under a charge of capital murder would be in error and automatically overturned on appeal. I couldn't contain the feeling of utter joy in making such a discovery. I asked my attorney how the surviving victim felt about me making a plea agreement for a life sentence. I learned that he agreed with the plea bargain. Although the charge was reduced, I would still be under an aggravated sentence in light of the judge entering an affirmative finding of a deadly weapon. Without the aggravated circumstances, I would have been up for parole immediately. I, on January 13, 1993, accepted a life sentence for 1st degree murder. And now I would join the prison population.

CHAPTER XXXII

ROCKIN' ROBERTSON.

In 1993, I was assigned to a fairly new unit, the French Robertson unit in Abilene, Texas. This unit acquired the name Rockin' Robertson in regards to all the violence that occurred on the unit. My first night there, I witnessed a man holding his bloody head as he sought help from the officers.

Within the prison, there are minimum, medium and maximum custody levels of the maximum security unit. I was assigned to the minimum part after a night in medium custody. I was now required to have a cell partner. We were allowed to have cell partners on death row, but that was by choice after being classified to be on the work program. The cell partner matter was different in population for me because when the majority discovered that I was a former death row inmate, they would become a bit paranoid whereas they would be extra kind to me to prevent causing me anger. I had one inmate tell me that others had asked him how could he live with me knowing that I had been on death row. He explained that he expressed to them that I was a good person, but he would definitely pack up and leave if we'd ever got into an argument even though such would result in him receiving a disciplinary infraction for refusing housing.

The mentality was that if you've been on death row, something is seriously, psychologically wrong with you. I sought transfer from this unit in order to get away from all the violence surrounding me. I had witnessed a man being jumped on by an officer, the man was in handcuffs behind his back. And it was like a daily occurrence to see someone bloody, or hear about someone being stabbed. Many of the fights were of officers and inmates.

I didn't have any interest in studying to obtain my education while on death row. "What could education do for a man who was about to die?" was my attitude. I enrolled in school on the Robertson unit, primarily to escape doing field work, and in order for me to stay in school I was required to take tests. After taking one of the tests, the teacher informed me that my score was high enough to qualify me to

take the GED. What did I have to lose? I passed
everything except the math, which encouraged
me to study math, the subject I hated the most.
I eventually passed and immediately enrolled
in college. I had never dreamed of achieving
this accomplishment. I enrolled in computer
literacy class, but the unit discontinued their
college program, thus, allowing me to seek a
transfer. In August of 1996, I was transferred
to the Alfred D. Hughes unit. This unit would
become more than just a prison.

CHAPTER XXXIII

OUT OF THE GRAVE.

The atrocities of life distort the perception of those potentially capable of achieving something of value, leaving them mentally shackled and chained by horrific occurrences of the past. Occurrences that provoke permanent decisions in present situations, under temporary circumstances, which always pave the road to self-destruction; The road I traveled which led me into the outer darkness of living beyond the grave drenched in alcoholism, covered in the smoke of marijuana, wallowing in perverted sex, cruising the pages and movie theaters of pornography, swallowing the bitter pills of uppers and downers and psychiatric drugs in order to escape the torment I was experiencing psychologically, failing to realized that I was making matters worse. I was allowing what I had endured to affect my decision making, which produced negative results that literally kept me physically shackled and chained to my additions and locked behind the wire of incarceration.

Often the horrors of the past are used as excuses to continue in negativity.

"If this person or that person had not done that to me, I wouldn't be doing this!"

Many have endured physical abuse in toddler and or adolescent stages of life who now use it in adult stages as an excuse to assault. There are those who endured molestation and being violently raped who now use it as an excuse to indulge in homosexuality, prostitution, lesbianism, and illicit sex.

Those who have endured psychological abuse now use it as an excuse to be manipulative. Some of these same horrific experiences have been used as an excuse to rob, steal, kill and destroy.

For a great deal of my life I played the blame game as my excuse. I blamed my mother and father, whose attention I vigorously craved, for walking out on me. I blamed my stepbrothers for jumping on me and ridiculing me, I blamed everybody that caused me grief for my bad choices, however, the moment comes when it is time to stand up and take responsibility for our own actions.

The torment of my soul began to rise to send the tears of my shame I've endured and experienced streaming down my face. I sought to find definition and affirmation because my identity was lost in my hiding. I had gone into hiding because I was afraid of being who I was told I would be —nothing! which sent me into hiding from myself, but I turned out to be who I had no desire to be: a liar, gambler, conniving, perverted, a thug, robber, thief, a drunk, drug addicted, vindictive, manipulative, hateful, suicidal and yes, even a *murderer*. The tears of my torment cried out,

"LORD! my soul is crying out to you!"

I had desired to do better in different stages of my life, but it was impossible of my own volition, I needed something or someone greater than myself to bring me out of the depths of my torment.

All my life I'd heard about God and how He sent His only begotten Son to die for my sins. On many occasions I had been to church, ushered in the church, sang in the church, played the drums in the church, but the church was not in me. Matter of fact, I was in church when the tears of my torment rolled down my face. I was drowning, sinking in the sea of wickedness, but a despairing cry was heard and the lifting process of my rescue went into immediate affect thereafter.

It was a warm May evening while cruising the corridors of the prison. An officer stopped me and told me that he had been watching me. I had been dodging him like he had the plague because I knew he was a Christian, and I had no desire to take Christianity serious, there was too much wickedness to give up that I felt a need to hold on to. But there was something special about this night.

He told me that I had the anointing upon me and that God called me to preach. He began to share with me how God worked a miracle in his life by raising him from the dead. He shared with me how he had parachuted out of a plane during his time in the military, but his parachute malfunctioned. He had been pronounced dead on the scene of his landing. I was captivated and interested in all he had to share with me, which was unusual. I've never considered talking to any officers unless I was pursuing to get some contraband out of them. He had a lot more to offer then I've ever anticipated in my life. At one point, the officer began to hesitate to share with me and stated, "man, I can't be talking to you like this, I'm an officer at work," but I was like a hungry lion feeding on his catch.

Although his statement in connection with me preaching was stunning, it was interesting because I've heard this statement many times before as I was growing up. My grandmother told me that I would preach as well as some of her Christian friends. I had even, surprisingly, heard the same statement from Joyce.

The officer further told me that I would have a big ministry when I get out.

About two hours later as I was walking toward my housing area, tears commenced to stream down my face uncontrollably. I was being chased by the Holy Ghost. As I was walking down the prison corridor I remember thinking that if my friend, who is a Christian, had his cell door open, with the light on and his cell partner was in the dayroom, I would immediately go to his cell to ask him to pray for me. When I got there, he was alone and as I approached him I began to cry again, but I managed to ask him to pray for me.

All of what the officer had told me was confirmed. One of the chaplains, out of the blue, called me during a church service and told me that he wanted me to have a "preacher's bible." He stated that I would have to recite the first chapter of James. He would tell the congregation every week how to obtain this bible and I would say to myself that that's a bible I would never get if I had to memorize scripture, but all of a sudden I had a hunger for the Word of God and to memorize James 1. I paced the floor in the dayroom, in my cell, on my job in the law library until I had the chapter in my heart. One Sunday morning I quoted James 1 to the chaplain to obtain my new "Believer's Study Bible"

One man told me thereafter that he could see the Holy Ghost on me. Another told me that he had a premonition and that there was something big for me.

In June of 1997, the following month, I accepted Jesus as my Lord and Savior. I don't remember the exact night I accepted Christ because I was in a state of shock at what had happened. I was on my knees praying to God asking that He allow me to feel His presence. Before I could complete the word presence, I felt this warmth as though something was being poured upon me. It went from the crown of my head to the soles of my feet.

Prison had now become more than prison —it was now my seminary.

I had heard on many different occasions that I would preach but I wanted to hear it from God. About three days later as I was asleep on my bunk, I heard this voice gently speak, "PREACH! PREACH! PREACH!"

Although I hadn't been good to myself, God has always been good to me, even in spite of me turning my back on Him.

I spent a great deal of time desiring to matter and mean something to someone, but I found that I mattered and meant something to the someone who I purposely failed to consider. Even though I was ridiculed, reproached and restless, I was being restored. Even though I experienced hopelessness, helplessness, hinderances, I was being healed. Even though I was a liar, lost and lonely, I was loved. Even though I experienced depression, desperation and deceitfulness, I was being delivered. Delivered out of the grave that I may direct those with the same and or similar experiences, to safety.

You don't have to allow what is adversely affecting you to have control over you which has sent you into the experience of graveyard living. You don't have to live up to other peoples' expectation, nor do you have to live under what others prescribe for you out of their insecurities, inconsistencies and inadequacies. You don't have to be ashamed. You don't have to go into hiding for the purpose of being someone you're not because you're ashamed of who you are. You don't have to live in fear. You don't have to continue in failure. You can live above what you've lived below for far too long.

You can come out of your graveyard living.

The voice of the one you've ignored is calling! It was there in the tomb of my life that I was directed to "COME!" Although I had been wrapped in the messes of life, my bonds were loosened, and I have escaped. I had given up on living just as others had given up on my life, but I have found that life had just begun. Out of the grave I came to find peace, love, joy, and happiness. Out of the grave I've found victory. I can hold my head up. I've found that I am somebody. I'm more than a mere existence, I'm more than a conqueror! Out of the grave I've discovered that I'm an over-comer. I've found that the grass is greener, the sky is bluer, and life has purpose! Out of the grave I've found salvation!!!

With salvation comes revelation. There are many escapes from danger, unbeknownst to us, that are revealed after salvation.

As I sat in the dayroom during mail call, I received a letter from someone I maintained contact with. He was still on death row. In his letter, he informed me that his lawyer failed to file documentation regarding his case. I thought he would be alright. The courts must allow her to straighten the matter out, I thought. I had considered my own state of affairs when I was sitting in the death watch cell on Ellis. "My attorneys would straighten everything out."

A few days later a young man informed me that someone had just been executed. I went to the library to seek finding out whether or not it was the young man I maintained contact with.

It was him.

His photo was on the cover of a San Antonio newspaper, contributing to sending tears to stream down my face. "Wow! I was trusting my attorneys in that death watch cell when in fact I should have been trusting God," I said to myself.

There definitely has to be something more to life than I anticipated. I must exist to a greater extent that God would want me to continue in life when on many fronts I wanted to give up.

CHAPTER XXXIV

DUNGEON BOY.

I've learned that freedom is an internal achievement as opposed to an external suggestion, whereas, we associate being in freedom's light with being totally free. We can live in freedom's light yet still be incarcerated. Living under what others prescribe for us is a form of incarceration. Addiction is still another form of incarceration. Living life without accepting Christ is the worst form of incarceration and it would be ironically counterproductive to spend one's life incarcerated, then die and as a result have to spend eternity—incarcerated!

When I accepted Christ, I received freedom from my addictions, lack of self-esteem, and parental abandonment. Yet, most of all, I received freedom from the psychological abuses that continually wreaked havoc in the caverns of my soul. I had never entertained the thought that anyone could convince me to divulge what tortured me the most. One of my attorneys had sought to get information from me to implement in my appeal to try and convince a court to release me from death row which would reveal some form of trauma, mitigating to the charges of capital murder, but my past experience was too embarrassing to release from my tortured soul. I had determined that this would definitely go to the grave with me.

One day as I sat in the A-D. Hughes unit chapel, a major of the Dallas salvation army stood before the church congregation to testify about what he had witnessed when he was visited by a woman and her small son.

She had reported that the little boy was being abused by his step-father.

Even though his mother realized this was happening, she continued to allow her son to live under those conditions; the major could see that the little boy was being physically abused when he removed the little boy's shirt. I fought to prevent the tears from streaming down my face as I visualized the torment the little boy would experience in his life because of the abuse if its never dealt with psychologically, but my teary fight was lost when the major mentioned investigating further. The major had removed the boy's pants as he stood him atop his desk and made the most horrifying discovery. The little boy's rectum was ruptured from sexual abuse; molested by his step-father.

Although I had never seen the boy, I held his condition in my heart. In my mind I screamed out to this child to take him in my arms to let him know that I'll protect him.

Manhood lives in the mansion of childhood, the place where joy and happiness reign. Where peace, love, laughter or a simple smile radiate to affect those who come in contact with them. This mansion is where hate is unheard of and racism is unseen, that is until a victimizer burglarizes the child's habitat to pour from the cup of wrath brimstone of destruction, which provides definition to adversely affect the psychological make-up of the child to shove him into adulthood to function in a state of perversion; to function in a state of destruction.

The little boy's story took my thought into the dank and dark corridors of a dungeon, a dungeon I had built.

There I visited a similar little boy. A boy who had found himself in the clutches of Mr. Lust in broad open daylight, in a Dallas drainage ditch—molested!

Raped of a normal life.

That-little boy was me, molested by a man in the neighborhood who I trusted.

I had believed in the man. I thought he was interested in being my friend, but he turned on me, he tricked me, he trapped me. I thought he was the one I could look up to, the one I could count on, who would look out for me. Instead, I found him looking down on me in his lust. I wanted to scream for help but who would hear? Who would take the time? Who would face up to this man? Paralyzing fear struck me a physical blow relaying the message to my mind that my victimizer would and could hurt me even more if I struggled.

The fear of what anyone would think to see me in this predicament held me bound.

I was afraid that if someone came to my rescue they would ridicule me. I was in a state of confusion. I laid there hoping that it would soon end but it has lasted me my whole life,

taking me into the war zones of life to
terrorize, tantalize and victimize.

Physical and psychological pain attacked me in
their demonic form as I walked down the street
with my rapist's semen in my underwear.

The demons tore at my heart with gnashing
teeth and claw like fingernails in a feeding
frenzy that would put sharks to shame.

I felt like I was bleeding to death. I ignored
neighborhood friends trying to invite me to
visit them in childhood. Childhood was over
with. Besides, I feared that they would
discover what I had just endured by their
questions and inquisitive glances.

The short walk home was long and painful in
itself and upon my arrival I discarded those
semen stained underwear in a field in the back
of the house where my grandmother and me
lived and locked that ten year old little boy in
the dungeon of my soul and buried him in the
deafening sound of silence later to feed him
with drugs, alcohol, illicit and perverted sex as
the matter has on many occasions replayed in
my head, visualizing the scene and the
degeneration of the man's satisfied lust quickly
turning into hate, "And you better not tell
nobody!" he warned.

226

As I sat in the crowd assembled in our chapel, I came face to face with my own little dungeon boy cowering in the far dark corridor of my soul. I cried out,

"I'm sorry little boy! I'm sorry I left you here all these years, caged, chained, bound and malnourished. I'm sorry I left you here crying, screaming, kicking, shouting, and cursing. I'm sorry I left you here in a fit of rage to torture yourself and terrorize others. No one came to your rescue. No one gave you any attention, not even me."

"Shhh… hush little boy! Tell no one," I told you.

"I couldn't allow anyone to see your ugliness. People would laugh at you and scorn you. They would associate what you've endured with homosexuality and ridicule you as a homosexual.

They will avoid you, curse you, hush little boy!'"

The ugliness had manifested itself in my flawed behavior.

"Look, little boy. I've brought a new friend. His name is Jesus. He has come to release you. He has come to comfort you, He has come to relieve you of your fears, your torment, your hurts; He has come with healing in His hands. He will not laugh at you or ridicule you. He will not use you or abuse you. Neither will He deceive or discourage you. He will not abandon you, nor will He denounce you.

He is a true friend that will stick closer than your brother. When you cry, He will wipe away your tears, when you're hurting, He will ease your pain. To you He will be all you need!"

The rusty chains of confinement held its grips, refusing to release the little dungeon boy who had become trapped in the confines of the occurrence, but Jesus' gentleness remained.

Into His arms Jesus took the little dungeon boy, Toby. "But what can you do with me now Jesus?" he cried. "After all I've experienced, after all of my terrorizing, after all of my wickedness, what use could I be to you when I've never been any use to myself? What use when I failed at so many things? What use..."

But Jesus looked beyond what I had become to see who I could be. He looked beyond my faults, frailties and failures to see my need.

He cleansed me, and delivered me.

When I fail to guard my heart and allow the evils of my past to return, He loves me through it and set my feet back in place and put them in motion. I've discovered that all along,

Jesus was all I needed.

CHAPTER XXXV

THIS IS PERSONAL.

My desire to read and study the word of God
was burning like an inferno. My first impulse
was to being in the New Testament because I
thought the Old Testament was obsolete, I
expressed to someone. Their response was,
"Why would God allow it if it was?" Okay, that
made sense. Since I had a hunger, I decided,
that I would start at the beginning and read to
the end. I had only read a scripture from time
to time, usually when my aunt or grandmother
requested me to do so, but now I was getting
into it for myself. I needed to know more
about this God who manifested Himself to me
on the most beautiful summer's night in my
life. My grandmother had told me about Him,
my aunt told me about , Him, other people told
me about Him, I'd heard preachers preach
about Him, I even imitated the preacher
preaching about Him when I was a boy. I'd
heard singers sing about Him. I had seen
people praying to Him, shouting before Him,

crying out to Him. Without knowing Him I had prayed to Him, shouted before Him and cried out to Him when I was in trouble. I'd seen people lifting their hands to Him. I'd seen people dance before Him but now this thing was personal. I needed to know Him! I needed to establish a personal relationship with Him.

He had faithfully stepped into my life. He got into my life when I didn't want to fully give up all my wickedness although my soul had cried out to Him. He had gradually changed my heart from my wickedness. I started losing the desire for it because I felt I was displeasing Him, that I was hurting Him. This thing was definitely personal. He had written to me a long letter—the Bible. I was lost in it. My understanding was cloudy, but I continued my journey. Some of His letter I found boring, but my desire to know Him superseded what I found boring, therefore, I pressed on. I had tried reading along with the "Read the Bible in a Year" instructions, but their process was too slow. God had reveal Himself good in order that I might know without a shadow of doubt that He was indeed a good God!!! I had fallen in love. It had to be love that sent me into the sanctuary to lift my hands without shame as tears flowed down my face in the midst of the congregation.

It had to be love that drew me into forgiving all the people who had caused me hurt, to seek forgiveness, from those I caused to hurt, more than that, to forgive myself. It had to be love to cause me to pay my tithes and offerings and give alms to others behind these prison walls who are without.

It had to be love to cause me to cease eating for days for the purpose of fasting in order to seek more of Him.

The desire to indulge in wickedness commenced to dissipate with each new day. I would literally see demons as dark shadows leaving me when I open my eyes after prayer.

My trip through the Bible didn't make much sense, so I began my journey again. This time I would take notes.

I learned that the whole Bible did matter, that in order to better understand the New Testament one must first get into the old because a great deal of the old is in the new. I discovered that the Old Testament is a natural manifestation of what we'd endured and have to endure in the spiritual. In other words, if you have a desire to understand your spiritual matters clearer, the Old Testament allows you to see it from a natural perspective.

More than that, I've learned that Jesus is in the Bible from Genesis to Malachi, from Matthew to Revelations. I discovered that He was the cool that walked in the garden with Adam and Eve.

He was the ark that rested afloat an angry sea in the days of Noah. He was the Angel that Jacob wrestled with until the break of day, the sacrifice that took Isaac's place on the altar in the days of Abraham, the tree cast in bitter waters that made the waters sweet, the bread that rained from heaven.

He was the Rock in a weary land that sprung forth water, the pillar of cloud leading the children of Israel by day and the pillar of fire leading them by night in Moses' day. He was also the rod in Moses' hand. He was the scarlet cord hanging from Rahab's window to redeem the Israelite spies in Joshua's day. He was the strength in Samson, the kinsman-redeemer in the days of Ruth, the oil that anointed David King, the stone that David used to bring down the giant. He was the wisdom given to Solomon, the praise that went forth to set

ambushes against Israel's enemies in the days
of Jehoshaphat, the book that Ezra opened that
caused the people to stand, lift their hands,
bow their heads and worship the Lord with
their faces to the ground.

He was the good that overcame evil in the days
of Esther, the restoration in Job's day. He was
the suffering servant in Isaiah's day, the tears
of the weeping prophet in Jeremiah's day. He
was the glory that filled the temple in Ezekiel's
day, the fourth man in the fire with Hananiah,
Mishael and Azariah; the hand that held the
lion's mouths closed when Daniel was cast in
the lions den.

He was the redeeming love expressed in
Hosea, the promise of the outpouring spirit in
Joel's day, the message of the coming
judgment in the days of Amos, the vengeance
in Obadiah's day, the mercy to the gentiles in
the days of Jonah, the much that came out of a
little in Micah's day, the yoke destroyer in the
days of Nahum, the tablet on which the vision
was written in the days of Habakkuk, the was,
the is, and the soon coming king who would
rule the nation, my personal savior, the Rose of
Sharon, trusted prophet, reigning king,
faithful scribe, redeemer that ever liveth,
burden bearer, miracle worker, sin bearer,

blessed hope, friend that sticketh closer than a brother, balm in Gilead, Lord of Lord, King of kings ,the first and the last, the beginning and the end the Alpha and Omega; He is Jesus the resurrected son of God who died and rose again who is now sitting at the right hand of the Father interceding for the saints.

It wasn't until after I accepted Christ, after I got into the Word of God that I realize that life has purpose. And the reason why I never valued life was because I couldn't see no purpose in life. I also realized that although I was thirty-two when I accepted Christ, I had never entered into manhood. One of the primary ingredients to manhood is responsibility. I had never taken responsibility for any of the crimes I've committed. How could I have committed such horrible sins; such horrible crimes? My primary concern had been about me, myself and I.

I can point an accusing finger at the atrocities I've endured in life, and although the law consider the mitigating circumstances associated with a particular crime, I stand as a man to take responsibility for my own actions in spite of. And prayerfully seek to make amends for my actions.

This had definitely became personal!

CHAPTER XXXVI

HER BEAUTY

She kept her silky, silver, shoulder length, hair
neat as she would often visit the beauty salon.
But there was a beauty far greater than the
beauty in her hair or appearance. It was the
beauty she so lovingly possessed within the
warm depths of her heart.

Of all the complaints the world has to offer, I
never heard her express one although she
endured much to complain about. She had
experienced being a battered wife and denied
the opportunity to be the mother SHE so
desired to be to her two children because of it,
yet she kept her head up, soaring above her
past circumstances instead of allowing her past
to affect her present. She held no grudges or
displayed any hate toward anyone. She would
be forgiving toward anyone who expressed an
unkind word toward her or displayed hate for
her. She was a hard fighting woman and

would combat the wars of hate with love —the love of Jesus!

I don't know when my grandmother accepted Christ in her life, but she lived as a godly woman who kept me in church regularly, matter of fact, we practically lived in the church. On one occasion around 1972-73, we lived in a house in East Dallas where another portion of the house was a church.

I grew to dislike church in my adolescent stages of life because it would always interfere with me riding my bike, playing house with the little girls or just hanging out with other mischievous adolescences.

The first time, I recall, I pursued to get out of going to church is when one of my little friends' made me aware of how he got out of going to church by putting lead on a piece of paper in order to put around his eye to make it look like his eye was black. I tried it, but it didn't work. As I considered later in life, it wouldn't have made a difference with my grandmother. An ailment would get me in church faster because she believed in divine healing. If it was an ailment to cause me to be bedridden, she would have immediately went into prayer and fasting for my healing because earthly doctors were out of the question. If God couldn't do it, it couldn't get done.

When I was 6 or 7, I got stabbed in the head with steel kitchen utensil by another little boy for something I did to him in which I don't remember. The only doctor on my case was my grandmother's home remedy and her prayers.

 On another occasion I was food poisoned. My sickness was so near death that my grandmother, at one point, was on the verge of calling the morgue. She always believed that I had been raised from the dead because she told me that she could not feel my pulse. Nevertheless, she prayed. Whatever happened in life, under any circumstance, she would pray.

Anytime I got in trouble she would always be there in prayer.

As treacherous as I turned out to be, she always considered me to be her blessing, her baby. She had prayed to God for an opportunity to be the mother she never got the opportunity to be to her children. Then came me.

She would often, exuberantly, express how she would take me in the bathroom with her to change my diapers. One particular story she would tell is how she would take me into the bathroom with her at church.

She gave up her life for me as her life was dedicated to being there for me, but Grandmama, the woman who had became mama to me, had left time for eternity right before my capital murder trial proceedings.

The last time I spoke with her was when I was in McKinney. I had been transferred there due to the publicity on the case, referred to as a change of venue. During a telephone conversation, mama expressed, "baby, Mama is sick!" That was the first time Mama ever expressed being sick. She had been sick for years, but she refused to visit any doctors. She discovered somehow that she had cancer. Often times I would witness her spitting up what the cancer was eating up although it didn't occur to me at those times. She lived by faith!

She enjoyed working as a caregiver to the elderly, and on some occasions, she would live in other people's homes to take care of their elderly parents. Most of her money was used to provide for me and she would give the rest of it to my aunt in order to help her financially for the purpose of building more rooms on my aunt's home.

Mama simply wanted a place to watch me grow into manhood; a place she could die in peace. Although I hadn't entered into manhood, she died when I was 21 years old.

Although I wasn't there, I knew the night mama died. There was a presence that came into the cell that prompted me to verbally say that, "I've lost mama!"

Followed by a song, "Cherish the Life." The song seemed to play continuously for about thirty minutes. About three days later I was visited by my aunt. In her effort to prevent me from stressing because of mama's death, she brought her old friend and her friend's daughter. She sought to use them and her laughter to hide from me what I already knew. "Where's mama?" I asked

Her expression was one of regret. "Oh, baby, mama is no longer with us."

Although I was on my way to death row when mama died, I know she was proud of me. Not for what I've done in life, but for what she knew I would do after death row. It hadn't occurred to me until after I accepted Christ in my own life that mama was gifted in knowing the future.

And it didn't occur to me until years later that mama knew I would be in the Caddo Detention Center. On the day we left to the prison for the purpose of my aunt's friend visiting her husband when I was twelve, I tapped mama on the shoulder, as soon as she looked in my face she commenced to crying uncontrollably. She never told me why, but now, God was revealing things to me. She would often tell me that I would be a preacher, and while I was in the Marshall jail, she told me that God was going to work a miracle.

God had revealed it to her. Although she is no longer here, she yet continues to live —she lives in my heart! Mama's life in Christ serves as a witness to me. I would often reflect on mama's Christian living to assist me in mine, and I would especially need her witness for what was ahead. Distraction sought to hinder my progress.

CHAPTER XXXVII

DISTRACTED.

On the balcony of my Christian life, about three years after accepting Christ, I found myself distracted. Although I was involved with the ministry, my Christian life started to bore me. My flesh was starved for excitement. But I went further than I intended and stayed longer than I expected.

The Spirit of God in me desired the things of God, but the flesh desired to indulge in the things contrary to the word, will and ways of God. My flesh had become my greatest opponent.

I've often encountered people and heard testimonies how many bargained with God in relation to salvation. "Lord, if you get me out of this troubled, I'll serve you." I accepted Christ because I had ventured into the realization that I needed someone greater than myself to enter into life. Prior to my acceptance I merely existed without direction. My soul cried out! But now I had entered a battle with the strangest individual—me!

I had eventually become the choir director, a member of the drama team and member of the Minister for Christ team. As a result of becoming a member of the minister for Christ team, our instructor, Chaplain Roberts, who was instrumental in me joining the class, desired for us to pray and preach before the congregation. Our graduation would result in us receiving our minister's license. But now I have relinquished my position. Although I would continue as a member of the choir, I was on the verge of laying it all down. But God was still in control!

I had eventually started working in the chapel as a Support Service Inmate clerk, but the escape I had on my record from the boy's home contributed to my job lost. The system was required to make changes after seven men escaped from the Texas prison system. Although I had later received my Support Service Inmate status back, I was given a job cleaning up the building I was housed on. Although I had signed documents that notified me that I would be working at night, my shift was mysteriously changed to work during the day with a man who used the nickname Shakey. He was the man chosen to direct the choir. He had no choir directing experience, but he wanted to pursue it. And he wanted me to help him.

"I will stick by you and teach you all I know, but once I believe you can handle it without me, I'm gone." I told him.

I had eventually started making and drinking jailhouse beer, commonly known as hooch. And started selling cigarettes. Although I had been delivered from cigarettes, I would occasionally return to smoking when I was drinking. Cigarettes had become illegal in about '94-'95.

A sentence is controlled by the legislature. I was sentenced under what is called the 65th legislature. Under this legislature I was considered as a mandatory supervision prospect, which means that I would automatically be released to mandatory supervision in spite of a parole denial. Therefore, I would be required-to do a third of my sentence. Although my sentence is assessed at life, it is the same as if I received a sixty year sentence, which is how a life sentence is computed for parole review. This meant that in 2004, I would be released. Someone eventually expressed to me that mandatory supervision release is now non-existent, particularly for those with life sentences.

Although I didn't accept Christ with a bargain for release, the news cut me to the core and scattered my thoughts. "Prison is my life." I responded to myself.

Right before my conversion, I met a young woman that would come in with her church Christian House of Prayer. God had revealed to me that this would be my wife, but my thoughts were so scattered that I immediately lost sight of what God had revealed to me to the degree that I started searching for someone in prison with whom I could find a cell together and live happily ever after.

The intensity of my dilemma influenced me to perfect my fighting techniques. I befriended a young man who wears the name of Kung Fu and was given the book of Bruce Lee. Although I had previously learned a few techniques in boxing and karate, I didn't learn as much as I was getting from Kung Fu. He took me into mixed martial arts: karate, judo, muay thai boxing, jujitsu, and aikido. We would practice for hours on a daily basis. Although I had a few minor physical confrontations since my incarceration, I was now preparing to seriously hurting someone, if not kill them.

"What are you doing, Toby?" I would often question myself as I would practice my combos. This was crazy I realized, but crazy would get respect for me and my little family and keep everybody out of my business.

Through it all I never stopped praying and reading the word of God because deep within I believed that God would somehow deliver, it was just a matter of time. My dilemma was causing me discomfort. Not only was my flesh succeeding in the fight, the devil was after me.

On a few occasions I would wake up in the middle of the night struggling to move as darkness enveloped the cell, but each time I was able to call out, "In the name of Jesus! In the name of Jesus! In the name of Jesus!" and I would experience release and the darkness would dissipate.

No one, aside from God, could comprehend
the magnitude of my struggles, not even me.

CHAPTER XXXVIII

REC. YARD PREACHER.

Astray, I had gone yet I longed for home. I felt like the prodigal son. My experience was like giving up living in the mansion to experience the pig pen of life.

"It's just a matter of time," I had told myself. "Before the laws ride down on me." I had seen it on many occasions where men would abandon the church and find themselves in the midst of a crisis and run back to the church. I hadn't fully abandoned the church, but I was well on my way. "Lord, get me out of this mess before something tragic occurs!" Although I continued reading the Bible and praying, my heart grew cold because I failed to guard it. "Guard your heart with all diligence for out of it flows the issues of life," the bible says. I allowed a statement to penetrate my thinking. The negativity I heard influenced me to believe that I would never get out of prison. My salvation was not predicated upon getting out. Eventually, things started to head in the right direction, although the process commenced through a slightly painful situation.

My left knee had swollen and I requested to visit the infirmary for the problem. The doctor told me that according to the x-rays, he could find nothing but there was something obviously wrong, he noticed as he compared my knees to see that one was larger than the other. He provided me with medication and medical restrictions: no prolong walking or standing, no walking on wet and uneven surfaces, no climbing and bottom bunk restrictions. These restrictions effected my job as an Support Service Inmate orderly on the building which prevented me from having access to the whole building. I was given a job in the garment factory as a drapery operator. I acquired the skills of making different types of curtains and using different types of sewing machines. God had delivered me out of my situation but my heart remained wallowing in the pig pen.

A few Christian men started gathering on the passive recreation yard, A small rec. yard we were allowed to just hang out on. I eventually joined them. A lot more than I anticipated was there. We became like family. The superficial did not exist. We shared with each other what was affecting our Christian lives without shame of what we have and were experiencing, something most of the church has abandoned. We need to know that even in Christ, we have struggles, we fail with regards to seeking our own desires that are contrary to the word, will and ways of God, and for many of us, we consider throwing in the towel although we realize, without a shadow of doubt, that God has been extremely good to us.

God would often manifest Himself in our group of, normally, twelve men. We would meet around 1900 hours and stay out until 2100 hours. Since many of us were apart of the Kairos community, we would attend Kairos on Monday night, but when we returned to our housing area, we would go to the passive rec. yard from 2000 hours to 2100 hours for an hour of prayer. Tuesday, Thursday, Friday and Saturday were our nights to hear someone bring the Word. Sunday and Wednesday we would not go out because these were our church days, but exceptions were made if someone needed fellowship or was experiencing a problem. Each of us would take turns pick out a date for which we think we would be prepared to bring the Word. My preparation consisted of much bible research and on the day of preaching I would enter into extensive prayer and fasting; pacing the floor of my cell preaching before my imaginary congregation .

Shame had no place with us. We would often find ourselves crying out to God on our knees, embraced or holding hands. We song praises and worshipped God. We prayed, cried, stood with and for each other. We often enjoyed eating and laughter, but there were times it appeared as though we were each other's enemy, but before we left the rec. yard we would be in tearful prayer seeking forgiveness from God and each other. This fellowship was a tremendous help to me, attributing to me regaining consciousness.

Occasionally that old devil would show up to see what was going on and sometimes he would have the audacity to speak. He came out on one occasion to accuse me, claiming that the spirit told him that I was involved with homosexuality since I had been gathering with the brethren. "What spirt?" It was later discovered that he had been listening to some gossip. He talked about the people in leadership positions in the church being involved with sin in their lives as if he had a Heaven or Hell to put them in and he used this as an excuse not to go back to church instead of standing as a man to admit that he was angry with those of us who were still in the ministry after he was excluded due to a disciplinary infraction.

"Ain't nothing but a bunch of homosexuals and hypocrites down there," he protested.

On another occasion he claimed that he wasn't going to return to the yard because we weren't in agreement with him to lower our voices during our praising and worship. A non-Christian told him that we were being disrespectful to the group that would be out on the same rec. yard playing dungeons and dragons. The same men we would show love to through our offer of some of our meals, despite their belligerence. Our singing would last no more than 15-20 minutes. The yard was opened from 1900-2145 hours.

Although I understood that we wrestle not against flesh and blood, I struggled with the desire to slap one of those devils. These were the same people who were on the yard when Kung Fu and me would practice. Nothing was said because they knew it would only accomplish violence.

Our gathering got slack when the weather got cold yet although it was cold, we would occasionally go out to fellowship. Some of the normal group got moved. Eventually, I was the only one out of the group that remained living on that wing.

Although I continued to battle with my flesh and struggled with prison being my final destination, I'm continuing with God.

CHAPTER XXXIX

PAROLE!

Surprise wrapped my heart with warmth upon receiving notice of my parole interview. By this time, in 2004, I had accomplished twenty years imprisonment. I commenced to jumping, shouting and praising God just to receive the notice because it occurred to me that, where I had come from, the only time a parole interview occurs is when a parole officer is doing a Will relating to an execution date. During my interview, the parole officer informed me that he will make an attempt to acquire a reprieve. I knew the attempt would be feeble. But now, I was on my way to being considered for parole release.

By this time I returned to looking forward to my return to freedom's light. I could see that I had and have a lot to be thankful for because I was coming up for parole to be considered for release instead of being paroled in Texas in order to go to Louisiana to do time. I had still had the charges of arm robbery, burglary and kidnapping pending. The beautiful thing about it all is that I stayed on death row long enough for the statute of limitations to run out on the charges.

Prior to my interview, a young man, during one of our rec. yard fellowships, told me as tears streamed down his face that he had a word from God who told Him that, "If He could get you off of Death row, He can deliver you out of this prison." This was confirmed the very next day when an outside minister visited the unit. I hadn't seen him in months, but he approached me while my hands were lifted up in the sanctuary, eyes closed as tears were streaming down my face as the song, "No Weapon," was being ministered by another visiting minister. He stated, "God has freed you my brother."

While on my knees in prayer, I heard in my spirit man, "you've just made parole!" I had been believing God for parole through His divine revelation upon my pillow of slumber and through different godly people who would approach me after their vision or dream of my release. But now, God was speaking directly to my spirit man. While I was in the midst of this prayer, I heard an officer who was in the dayroom during mail call, call my name.

I later discovered that it was my parole answer.

I was a bit startled when I noticed that I had been set-off five years. That parole board wasn't going to see me again until 2009. The answer was contrary to what God had just revealed; contrary to what people were relaying as a message from God. As I reflect on the time of my conversion, I remembered —I didn't accept Christ in order for Him to deliver me out of prison.

He commenced to revealing that He would after my conversion. Because of the evidence I have, predicated upon what He has already done, I'm confident that He has it worked out in His perfect timing. And I have to always remember that had it not been for His intervention, I would never be considered for parole to return to freedom's light.

"For I know that thoughts I think toward you, says the Lord, thoughts of peace and not of evil, to give you a future and a hope "It had appeared that His thoughts were evil toward me, especially when the judge announced, you are hereby sentenced to death..." All hope had dissipated, I had no future. But all of that has been restored. Weariness often time visits and I have to remind myself that He has it worked it out. Then it occurred to me that He often has us under particular circumstances in order to work out of us what's not of Him in order that He may work in us what He will in order to get the best of Himself from us. And in many situations, the purpose is for others to see how we respond to unpleasant news as people of God.

Although my departure regarding parole had not arrived, my departure from the Hughes unit for educational purposes had.

CHAPTER XL

MOTIVATIONAL SPEAKER

Often we have a tendency to travel life's journey defining ourselves as victims in regards to the victimization we've endured. Our self-worth is either diminished or depleted. And when we habitat in that particular building, we venture into being predators, seeking to victimize. There's truth to that cliché that says, "hurt people hurt people." But I've discovered that people who have been hurt have the potential to use the area of their hurt to help.

In the midst of all the Beto unit confusion and chaos, the avenue was paved for me to journey for the purpose of using the hurt I've endured to help. It commenced with a 60 year old, grey-haired, Caucasian woman who taught cognitive intervention. I had been permitted to go into the library during her class library time to meet a Christian brother I had befriended.

When their library time was up, I remained in order to find a book to check out. In the midst of my book search, the cognitive teacher and Christian brother returned.

"Hey, come here," she ordered as she stood in the entrance door of the library.

Believing I was on the verge of encountering a disciplinary infraction, I approached with caution.

"Come out here for a minute."

When I stepped in the corridor she simply asked, "you were on death row?"

"Hey, man, I didn't mean for her to say anything.", He tried to explain.

"It's all right. Yes, maam."

"Would you be interested in speaking to my class? I know you would have something to tell my class about life."

"Yes, ma'am."

"Write it up," she stated as she walked off.

Tell them about life, I thought. At this particular juncture in my life, I was struggling with the appreciation for life. Although I wasn't struggling with the issue of suicide as much, the thoughts were reoccurring in spite of my new life in Christ. Therefore, what could I possibly tell them, about life?

As I commenced to prepare for my talk, I begin to notice how much of our lives, mine in particular, are consumed by chasing the large and expensive things and neglect the things that are of value such as: meaningful relationships; family, above all, a relationship with Christ. I eventually began seeing how I had some contradictory issues. I can appreciate being fearfully and wonderfully made, capable of accomplishing much, yet have a lack of appreciation for life. But wait! There were other issues to surface. Although I sought to cease living up to others expectations, some remnants of the issue continued to linger based upon my perception of others regarding me.

Although I eventually recognized that I was hiding from me and my identity lost in hiding, I now discovered that my identity was in what I've endured. Therefore, I would perceive others feeling negative about me who never disclosed to me such. It was all predicated upon how I felt about me. Because of it, I discovered that I was basically living up to others expectations on another level. I was previously aware of what others expected and was living up to what they prescribed, but now I was living up to what I perceived others expected of me that was filtered through what I've endured which manifested that I was enslaved to what I've endured. And this manifested that I was lacking in faith as in biblical times regarding the children of Israel.

The children of Israel had been delivered from captivity; promised by God to experience a land flowing with milk and honey. After a few days journey after their miraculous deliverance, twelve men from each tribe were commanded to spy out the land of Canaan. When they returned, they manifested witnessing what they had been promised. The problem: ten of the twelve conveyed a bad report based upon their perception of themselves. "There we saw the giants (the descendants of Anak came from the giants); and we were like grasshoppers in our own sight..." Numbers 13:33, NKJV. They further stated, "and so we were in their sight." The problem with that is that the people of that place did not see them or there would have been fatalities. The evidence of this lie in Joshua 2 where the prostitute Rahab hid the spies because the people of that place discovered them and sought to kill them.

Although the people of Canaan had never seen them, they responded based on their slave mentality; based on their lack of faith. Therefore, their perception was not based upon how others relayed feeling about them, but based upon how they felt about themselves.

My first talk primarily revolved around being consumed by the chase of the expensive things which result in us missing out on the valuable things in life. The issue that would get their attention was the fact that I had been on death row. And their questions revolved around "How was it on death row?"

I had recognized how that I could use being on death row in the negative.

The stigma associated with being on death row is that you're mentally unstable; a killer. And there were times I felt I had to use it in order to divert an officer's attention who was harassing me and for the purpose of preventing someone I believed I would have trouble with from causing such. But now I discovered how it can be used on a positive level.

I had believed that my talk in the cognitive intervention class was my first and last, but the teacher had me to speak in other classes where I pretty much shared the same thing. After a period of time, she invited me to return to her class.

As the time for me to return to the cognitive teacher's class approached I begin to feel the pressure of not being prepared, but within was an unction

"Share that story." Share that story, oh Lord no! I thought. I can't share that story. They'll ridicule me and associate what I've endured with homosexuality. There's no way I can share with them the story of molestation!

But upon my second talk, a boldness overcame me, and for the first time in my life, I shared in detail how I had been molested at the age of 10 in a Dallas drainage ditch in broad open daylight.

As I shared the story, tears begin to stream down my face along with a few others, including the cognitive teacher. But in the midst, a problem surfaced. A young man who sat directly in front where I stood commenced to fidgeting to the degree that I was almost distracted, but I was able to press my way

264

though. Afterward, I spoke with a gentleman who was in class just to hear my talk how that I almost lost it because of the young man's fidgeting. His response was: "He probably was doing that because he could identify with what you've endured."

Wow! I had never thought of that and his response was confirmed. One day, while in church, after the service was over, I heard someone screaming my name. I saw him from a distance. It was the distracting young man. By the time he approached, he had tears streaming down his face and he relayed to me that: "I want to tell you something I've never told anybody. I've never even told my mama. When I was five years old, that happened to me."

And that's when I lost it. Tears begin to stream down my face and the reality of sharing "that story" struck. There was purpose behind what I've endured and for the first time I could see how I can use what hurt to help. What I've endured is not necessarily about me, but those who are like me; those who have experienced the same or similar. I therefore, made up in my mind that, in spite of the twinge of embarrassment I sustained in sharing the story, my concern for people would supersede the embarrassment. They needed me. And I came to the realization that I needed them, even if it wasn't but for having the opportunity to share "that story." And in doing so, I discovered that my own healing was being accomplished.

CHAPTER XLI

GRAVEYARD SECRETS.

A particular talk I enjoyed doing was entitled, "Graveyard Secrets." I've conveyed this talk on many occasions because I believe it was the most informative. I believed this talk was more influential in regards to the men delving into dealing with the atrocities they've endured in life.

My talk would normally begin like this:

 "Thank you for allowing me the opportunity to speak in your class once again. More than that, thank you for your concern for those of us who reside behind these walls of incarceration. Thank you for allowing me this moment in your lives where I hope I'm able to provide you with something you can find valuable for your lives, but that does not imply that I have it together, that I've arrived or that I know it all. None of us know it all, and I've recently come to the realization that we only know a partial bit of what we think we know, Why? because someone knows what we know to a greater extent. And there's a lot of things we claim to know that we really don't because much of that is based on misinformation. It is my belief that the most bitter bondage is the bondage of misinformation.

How many of you ever heard of the theory of cognitive dissonance? Cognitive dissonance is this: I can believe a lie for so long that that lie eventually operates as my truth. Later in life, when I am met by the actual truth, my mind automatically rejects the actual truth because I've adopted the lie to operate as truth.

For instance, many of us have experienced being told what we have to accomplish in order to enter into manhood. "Boy, you're not a man until you're working and paying your own bills." "You're not a man until you've had sex with a woman" , "you're not a man until you drink a certain type of alcoholic beverage."

The one I've been hearing lately that's appalling is, "you're not a man until you've gone to prison.

You never have to *prove* manhood.

"Now, I want to talk about Graveyard Secrets.

"One of our favorite pastimes behind these walls of incarceration is traveling the boulevard of reminiscing for the purpose of caressing those special moments with our memories. And to assist us in our journey, we'll invite others to cruise the pages of our photo album.

Words escape your lips, yet no one can hear you. Words escape their lips yet you can not hear them. The touch of the experience is evident, yet the emotions now refuse to feel. Yet lying under the soggy dirt secrets of this grave lie the greatest treasures.

"In 1984, I was arrested for aggravated armed robbery, burglary and one count of kidnapping in Louisiana. The charges of attempted capital murder and capital murder are in Texas. Under the charge of capital murder, one is considered insane until proven sane. Therefore, in order for me to escape going to death row, I need to remain according to law —insane! My plan was to serve the authorities with the meal of insanity. For my psychological evaluation, I was sent to Rusk Mental State Hospital, but while I was in Rusk, it occurred to me that every time I look around, I'm finding myself in situations like this. I started experiencing incarceration when I was about 12 or 13. Between that time up until I was 15, I had been locked up so many times that I lost count, finally at fifteen, I found myself locked up for attempted capital murder. As this occurred to me, that most famous question came to mind, why? Why do I continue to find myself in these types of situations?"

Why?

"Why are you here? My cognitive intervention teacher, Mrs. Carter, often states that we started coming to prison long before we got here. She makes this statement because she realizes that we were exposed to things in childhood that built the road which leads to prison. Be careful though, that once you discover this you don't use it as an excuse to continue in committing those same or similar crimes that got you here; playing the blame game for your justification."

When?

"In order to delve deeper into the investigative process, It's necessary to look at when. For instance: when I was 12 or when I was 14..."

(I would go into the story of the abandonment I experienced regarding my mother.)

Who?

"The when manifest the who. In this case my mother. Now, we're going to mark this area because we're going to have to deal with the who later."

What?

"The who manifest that what had been done. In my experience, that what is abandonment."

Where?

"Now, it would be necessary to ask ourselves, 'Is where am I as result of what happened?' It's not where you are physically, but where are you on a psychological level."

How?

"Once we make these discoveries, it's imperative that we seek to discover how we're going to prevent this from continuing to have an adverse psychological effect on us."

"In my Bridges to Life class, I was provided the opportunity to watch a powerful film along these lines. Two men were arrested and sentenced for the murder and rape of a young married mother. The mother and daughter of the deceased woman contacted a mediation service and made contact with one of the men. The other man had been declared insane, therefore, she was not allowed to make contact with him. After a short correspondence period, the mother and daughter of the murder woman were allowed a contact visit on the Allred unit. They faced the man responsible.

"After sharing a bit of their life's experience, the mother wanted to know what were the last words of her daughter. He stated that her last words were,

'I forgive you!' The tears of her last words streamed down each of their faces. For about five to ten minutes they cried. But what happened next floored me. The mother looked the man straight in the eyes as she held the hands responsible for murdering and raping her daughter and relayed to him, "I forgive you too. And when you come up for parole, I will have no problem in you making it."

Forgive

"This is where we're going to have to deal with the *who* The forgiving the who is more about you. Holding on to unforgiveness is like drinking poison and expecting someone else to die.

"Forgiveness can be difficult but look at it from this perspective, Have you desired the judge and or jury to show mercy to you in spite of the harm you caused? Or have you desired the parole board to show you mercy when you come up for parole? Our desire to receive mercy from them is basically our desire to be forgiven by them. Therefore, why do we experience difficulty when it comes to forgiving? One of the things I've discovered is that the reason many of us have difficulty in forgiving is because we haven't forgiven ourselves. But that poses a question. How do you forgive yourself?"

First: "you forgive yourself by taking responsibility for your own actions. Now, I realize that there are some contributing factors involved, but in spite of what happened to me that contributed to my adverse decision to commit some type of atrocity, I stand as a man to take responsibility for my own actions. Taking responsibility is the primary ingredient to manhood."

Second: "you forgive yourself by recognizing that what happened to you was not your fault. Many of us blame ourselves for our own hurt. 'If I wouldn't have went over there, he wouldn't have done that to me.' Or 'if this wouldn't have happened, that wouldn't have happened.'

"I want to use a particular film to convey this, entitled "The Heart of Texas." This lady was driving down the street with her two children in the back of their van. A commotion ensued to the degree that the mother had to pull over to the side of the road. As soon as she stopped, the little girl opened the door and got out of the van. She was struck by a truck, as it was later discovered. The man that hit her didn't know he ran over the little girl.

Later, on another day, the little boy conveyed to his mother that had he and his little sister hadn't been arguing over a toy, she wouldn't have died.

The mother's response was powerful. She told the little boy to get the toy. When he returned with the toy, she further conveyed that they were going to blame it on the toy, Iit's the toy's fault.' She provided him with a hammer and told him to take the toy to the edge of the drive way for the purpose of breaking the toy. She said that he had toy parts all over the yard. What she did for him was transfer the blame because he was about to travel life's journey blaming himself for what happened to his little sister. And whenever we blame ourselves for anything we've done in life, we'll find difficulty in forgiving.

"Forgiving ourselves prevent us from traveling life's journey being bitter."

"Not only are we required to forgive, it goes even deeper. We must forget.

Forget

"We forget, not in the sense we don't remember what happened. What happened is our story. We forget in the sense that we don't allow what happened to continue to have an adverse effect on us. And once we've made this accomplishment, it is important for us to maintain our focus."

Focus

"Our choice to forgive and forget is daily, therefore, it's important that we seek to maintain our focus on what we've done.

"Have you ever played a game of chess where you had the advantage; a couple of moves from having your opponent in checkmate, yet you wound up losing the game? What happened is that you lost focus. You were so focused on offense that you forgot to maintain your focus on defense. Normally when losing a major piece, we give up, we throw in the towel. Now understand this, the person we're playing had lost their focus somewhere along the way.

That allowed us to have the advantage, but in spite of what was working against them, they stayed in the fight of the game. It's important that we maintain a fighter's attitude and stay in the fight."

Fight

"It's important that no matter what it looks like, stay in the fight. A fighter is not just a fighter in the ring, he's just as much of a fighter outside of the ring as he is inside. What he does outside of the ring determines his performance inside the ring. Outside the ring he's required to maintain a healthy diet, he's required to get proper rest and exercise.

There was a fighter by the name of Cassius Clay who fought Sonny Liston for the heavyweight champion bout. In the middle of the fight, Clay got this substance in his eyes that when he returned to his corner, the throwing in of the towel was discussed. Nevertheless, Clay returned to the fight for the purpose of fighting his way through. He finds himself on the ropes suffering unnecessary blows, he's down in points, but in spite of what he had working against him, he yet had something working for him. He was in the fight! Well, his staying in the fight resulted in him prevailing, he became the new heavyweight champion. Sometimes you may find yourself on the ropes of life suffering the unnecessary blows, where it seems as though every time you take one step forward, you seem to take two or three steps backward. But in spite of what you have working against you, you have something working for you by staying in the fight. If you don't know the fighter as Clay, perhaps you recognize him as Ali. In spite of his passing, many of us still recognize him as one of the greatest fighters of all times, and many of us recognize him as the greatest.

PURPOSE

"Many of us don't know our purpose. What is your purpose? When we fail to recognize our purpose in life, we'll eventually have a total disregard for life and the livelihood of others. Personally, I believe that our purpose derives from what we've endured. The purpose of my story is to convey to others that are going through what I've been through in order that they may know there's a way out of what they're going through."

Although often in life that it does not appear that God has a matter under control, I am a witness that He does. I remember thinking at the time of my arrest, "It's over." But that was because I was looking at my circumstances by sight instead of by faith. Whenever we look at a matter by sight, we have a tendency to look into the matter in regards to what we expect to get from it. And this is the reason many of us make such statements as 'I'm hoping for the best, but expecting the worse'. It's important that we walk by faith in spite of what it looks like.

In spite of all I've endured; in spite of a prison sentence, I made some accomplishments I never dreamed.

My college enrollment allowed me to study Human Resource Management, Philosophy, COBAL Computer Programming and Development Math. I've acquired a Windham plumbing trade, Central Texas College trade in Auto Mechanics and a, of course, Trinity Valley Community College trade in Computer Aide Drafting. I've received a Bible Study Diploma from Zion Faith College, an Associate's Degree in Religious Education, a Bachelor's Degree in Divinity and presently have twenty-nine credits toward a Masters Degree in Biblical Counseling from Shalom Bible College, Magna Cum Laude. I've

278

acquired certificates in classes: Bridges to Life,
Peer Health Education, Cognitive Intervention,
Experiencing God and Christian Believers and
a Certificate of Completion through
correspondence, Studies in Grace. I've also
received on-the-job training as a Cloth
Spreader and Drapery Operator.

I've always had the potential to accomplish
more, first and foremost, because I'm fearfully
and wonderfully made by a loving God.

I just couldn't see it until after I accepted
Christ.

I've been *redeemed*.

ABOUT THE AUTHOR.

Brother Toby is currently carrying out his life sentence in the Texas Department of Criminal Justice Beto Unit in Tennessee Colony, TX.

He goes up for parole review in February of 2018.

He invites anyone who has been touched by his story to write him:

TOBY LYNN WILLIAMS #631555

GEORGE BETO UNIT

1391 FM 3328

TENNESSEE COLONY, TX 75880